Primary Schools and ICT

D0658923

Also available from Continuum

Primary Schools and ICT

Learning from pupil perspectives

Neil Selwyn, John Potter
and Sue Cranmer

WITHDRAWN

BOWLING GREEN STATE
UNIVERSITY LIBRARIES

continuum

Continuum International Publishing Group

The Tower Building
11 York Road
London
SE1 7NX

80 Maiden Lane
Suite 704
New York
NY 10038

www.continuumbooks.com

© Neil Selwyn, John Potter and Sue Cranmer 2010

All rights reserved. No part of this publication may be reproduced or transmitted in any form or by any means, electronic or mechanical, including photocopying, recording, or any information storage or retrieval system, without prior permission in writing from the publishers.

Neil Selwyn, John Potter and Sue Cranmer have asserted their right under the Copyright, Designs and Patents Act, 1988, to be identified as Author of this work.

British Library Cataloguing-in-Publication Data
A catalogue record for this book is available from the British Library.
ISBN: 9781855395787 (paperback)
      9781855397514 (hardcover)

Library of Congress Cataloging-in-Publication Data
Selwyn, Neil.
    Primary schools and ICT: learning from pupil perspectives/Neil Selwyn, John Potter, and Sue Cranmer.
        p. cm.
    Includes bibliographical references.
    ISBN 978-1-85539-751-4 (pbk) – ISBN 978-1-85539-578-7 (pbk) 1. Educational technology–Great Britain. 2. Information technology–Great Britain. 3. Education, Elementary–Computer-assisted instruction–Great Britain. 4. Computers and children–Great Britain. I. Potter, John. II. Cranmer, Sue. III. Title.

    LB1028.3.S3888 2009
    372.133'4–dc22

2009034279

Typeset by BookEns Ltd
Printed and bound in Great Britain by CPI Antony Rowe, Chippenham, Wiltshire

Contents

List of abbreviations

BBC	British Broadcasting Corporation
C&IT	Communications and Information Technology
CBBC	Children's BBC (UK digital television channel for children)
CD	Compact disc
CD-ROM	Compact disc read only memory
CITV	Children's ITV (UK digital television channel for children)
DCSF	Department for Children, Schools and Families (UK government department with responsibility for schools in England)
ICT	Information and communications technology
INSET	In-service education and training
IT	Information technology
LA	Local authority
MMORPG	Massively multi-player online role playing game
MP3	Moving Picture Experts Group-1 Audio Layer 3 (name for computer files that use a particular digital audio encoding format)
MSN	Microsoft Network (colloquial name for Microsoft's instant messaging service)
Ofcom	Office of Communications
PC	Personal computer
PDA	Personal digital assistant
PR	Pupil researcher
PS2	PlayStation 2
PSP	PlayStation Portable
RSPCA	Royal Society for the Prevention of Cruelty to Animals
SAT	National curriculum assessments
SEN	Special educational needs
TV	Television

Acknowledgements

While responsibility for this book lies with its three authors, many people assisted us throughout the process of researching and writing.

First and foremost, we would like to thank the pupils and teachers who participated in the study. Without their participation and good humour we would not have any material for the book. We hope that you all benefited from taking part in the study.

This book derives from our work on a research project funded by Becta, the UK government's education technology agency. The views and opinions expressed in this book do not necessarily represent those of Becta. That said, we would particularly like to thank Diane Levine at Becta for her support throughout the project.

In terms of the process of putting this book together, we would also like to thank Bridget Gibbs for her work as Commissioning Editor at Continuum in working with us on the structure and content of the book. We would like to thank Susan Morse for her work on the transcription of the discussion groups and Michael Brown for data-inputting. We would also like to thank Daniela Boraschi for her work on the reproduction of the children's drawings in Chapter 6, and Suay Özkula for her help with the analysis of the drawings in Chapter 6.

Finally, we would like to thank our colleagues at the Institute of Education, University of London, for their advice and comments on the project – notably Diana Laurillard, Rebekah Willett, Ambrose Neville and Lynn Roberts. John Potter would like to thank Janet for interest, support and comments on the draft, and Alice and Jack for putting up with yet more iShed time. Sue Cranmer would also like to thank her husband Steve Griffiths for his interest in – and unfailing support for – this and all her other projects.

Preface

Unlike many other ICT books this is *not* a manual on 'how to use technology in the classroom'. In writing this book we wanted to take a step back from worrying about the dos and don'ts of using websites and whiteboards. Instead we were keen to address a rather trickier question about schools and technology – why is it that ICTs often seem to be an unexciting and uninspiring feature of primary education, despite all their potential? Above all, we wanted to use this book to explore the ways in which ICT use in primary schools could be improved, re-imagined and reinvigorated so that children and teachers no longer see the classroom as technologically inferior to the rest of their lives.

Although these intentions may have been ambitious, we hope that we have produced a realistic and insightful analysis of primary ICT. Unlike other authors writing on this topic, we do not believe that it is useful to apportion 'blame' on teachers or to identify personal deficiencies and barriers that are somehow 'causing' ICTs not to work as well as they should. If the use of ICT in a primary school is not as exciting or effective as it could be, then this can usually be traced back to a number of very understandable reasons. For example, any teacher hoping to make use of ICT in their classroom also has to contend with the numerous pressures of testing and assessment, the demands of meeting national curriculum requirements and the many additional labour-intensive priorities that are foisted onto schools each year. Given all these 'other' factors, even the most enthusiastic and determined of teachers would be justified in complaining that there is not enough time or space to squeeze ICT into the overcrowded environment of the primary classroom.

With these thoughts in mind we have tried to write a book which can act as a starting-point for rethinking primary ICT, and introducing innovative forms of ICT use 'around the edges' of the day-to-day priorities of the primary school. This is not an ICT book that makes hopelessly romantic calls for the abandonment of the primary curriculum or reinvention of the classroom. We are not so removed from the realities of schools and schooling that we advocate the abandonment of the timetable in favour of a technological 'free-for-all'. Instead, we have tried to reach suggestions for change that work with, rather than against, the current state of play in primary schools.

When thinking initially about how ICTs may be better integrated into primary education we decided on a rather unusual strategy. We felt that too many education technology writers begin by focusing on the latest technologies and marvelling over what these applications and tools are now technically capable of doing. Only much later is any thought given to how these technologies may possibly be inserted into existing classroom practice. This tradition of approaching new technology as a 'solution in search of a problem' has long dogged the use of ICT in schools. At the moment, for instance, the educational hype surrounding 'web 2.0' and 'web 3.0' tools illustrates how an over-zealous enthusiasm for all things high-tech can cloud the thinking of even the most level-headed of people. In fact we would argue that this 'technology-first' mentality is at the root of many of the problems and tensions experienced by teachers and pupils as they try to get to grips with the next 'next big thing' that has landed in their classroom. You will (hopefully) be relieved to hear that our book is deliberately *not* driven by a technology agenda.

As its title suggests, this book is also unusual in that our discussions are not driven by a teacher perspective. Although we take time in later chapters to listen to the views of teachers, ICT co-ordinators and school leaders, we chose to first pay close attention to primary pupils themselves and listen to *their* perspectives on how ICT is being used in schools. Given that teachers and parents often complain that they feel left behind by the technological know-how of children, it seemed that listening to young people's views and opinions on school ICT was an important first step to take.

With all these aims in mind we spent a year talking with – and listening to – primary pupils as they discussed what they do with ICTs in school and at home. More than 600 pupils were involved in our research project, talking through ideas and opinions amongst themselves, then debating these with adults, filling in surveys, making videos and (literally) sketching out ideas for future change. The wealth of information that we gathered from these pupils has helped us reach a number of often unexpected conclusions. From this basis we are able to offer some innovative recommendations for how ICT provision, policies and practices within schools can be tweaked and adjusted for the benefit of primary pupils and teachers alike.

So we hope that this book, if nothing else, will inspire educators to approach primary ICT in a slightly different way than before. In particular the ideas and opinions of the children in this book should remind adult readers of the benefits of thinking about technology and schools in a child-centred or even child-like way. Having completed our research project we are now convinced that there is real value in talking with and listening to children's views on the role of technology in their schools. We hope that readers are inspired to follow our lead. It may be that using children's ideas and perspectives can act as a powerful means of imagining what *could* and *should* be possible in the classroom. As one of the pupils in our book concluded:

> We had a teacher last year and she said when she was our age they fantasized about the things that we have now. And now we fantasize about the things that we might have in the future … I think it would be interesting to see if some of those things were actually coming true.

Neil Selwyn, John Potter and Sue Cranmer
London

The 'big' priorities and pressures of primary ICT

Overview: This chapter provides an overview of the growing significance of ICTs for primary education. It argues that primary ICT is subject to a set of 'big' priorities that often have little to do with the day-to-day concerns of teachers and learners. We start by considering the many reasons why primary schools are now compelled to be using ICT – not least the fast pace of technology development and the changing nature of children's digital lifestyles. We also consider the growing expectations of parents and policy-makers for a high-tech education system. We then describe how these priorities can put schools under a set of almost impossible pressures to make 'effective', 'engaging' and 'safe' use of ICTs. The chapter reaches the conclusion that whilst it is important for teachers and schools to be aware of these wider issues that drive ICT in education, it is important not to let them limit our ambitions when thinking of ways to improve primary ICT.

Introduction

Few people would disagree that information and communication technologies (ICTs) are an important part of the future of schools and schooling. In fact most people will have first-hand experiences of the potential of technologies to support and stimulate teaching and learning. Many parents have been amazed by the ability of the internet to bring their children into contact with information and resources that otherwise would be far beyond their means. Classroom teachers have long been impressed by the capability of the computer to manipulate data and allow it to be presented in a variety of ways. Many school lessons now benefit from the creative use of digital video cameras, handheld computers and other portable devices. Perhaps the most widespread classroom technology of the last ten years has been the interactive whiteboard – sometimes bringing lessons to life and stimulating whole classes of otherwise inattentive pupils.

Although educators are rightly justified in expecting great things from new ICTs, it is important to retain a sense of perspective. We should remember that education has a long history of waiting for technology to revolutionize the classroom. The educational expectations for current ICTs echo the last fifty years of largely unrealized predictions of a computerized 'revolution' in the classroom. Ever since Patrick Suppes' description of the imminent overhaul of teaching through the 'computer tutor' in 1965, many people have been awaiting a technological transformation of schools.[1] The 1970s and 1980s saw much excitement in educational circles about 'micro-electronics' and home computers. The 1990s was dominated by talk of new forms of 'virtual schooling' based around interactive video and the 'information superhighway'. In the 2000s excitement was reserved for interactive whiteboards and web 2.0 technologies. Now as we enter the 2010s, some educators are already beginning to talk about the potential of the 'semantic web' and web 3.0.

Fifty years on from the first flushes of enthusiasm for educational computing, ICT now displays the outward signs of being a high-profile, well-funded and well-resourced element of contemporary education. Yet although the appearance of technology in schools may have altered immensely during the past ten years, in many ways it could be argued that very little *fundamental* change has taken place. In spite of the enormous amounts of money directed towards it, ICT has somehow contrived to remain a superficial aspect of school life, always there but never really a central part of teaching and learning. Some commentators have said that schools' ICT is caught in a 'high access, low use' paradox where new technology continues to be a high-profile but, in practice, often symbolic element of 'modern' teaching and learning.[2] A few educationalists are even beginning to openly question the value of ICT resources in comparison to hiring additional teaching staff or buying more textbooks.[3] As Michael Apple concluded bluntly, perhaps it should be acknowledged by everyone in education that they have been simply 'wasting money on computers in schools'.[4]

We therefore start this book from a realistic rather than romantic point of view about ICT and schools. In particular, we approach ICT as being a cause both for celebration and for debate as far as primary educators are concerned. While we should remember that ICT is a potentially good – if not great – thing for schools, we cannot assume that it will simply 'come right' of its own volition. As Diana Laurillard reflected recently:

> education is on the brink of being transformed through learning technologies; however, it has been on that brink for some decades now.[5]

As this quotation implies, there is certainly much room for improvement if the potential benefits of new technologies in schools are to be realized on a widespread and sustained basis. This book is therefore concerned with how to best go about changing ICT use in primary schools in a realistic and reasoned manner. This opening chapter sets the scene for the whole book by discussing exactly what ICT is and precisely why schools are expected to be making best use of it.

What do we mean by 'ICT'?

Technology is an area of life where jargon, abbreviations and technical terms abound – often causing much confusion and annoyance to anyone who is not especially interested in the difference between a 'byte' and a 'bit', or a 'tweet' and a 'poke'. In this sense, although the different terms used in education to refer to new technology are not especially complex, they can lead to unnecessary confusion. Before we can start discussing primary ICT in earnest, it makes sense to take a little time to first consider what is meant by the deceptively short, three-letter abbreviation 'ICT'.

Put simply, this book is concerned with the use of digital technologies by pupils and teachers in primary schools. By 'digital technologies' we are referring to a range of different aspects of contemporary technology use:

- computing hardware (such as desktop PCs, laptop computers, interactive whiteboards);
- personal computing devices (such as mobile phones, personal digital assistants, MP3 players);
- games consoles and handheld games machines;
- 'content-free' computer software packages (such as word-processors, spreadsheets);
- 'content-related' computer software packages (such as simulation programs, tutorial packages);

- world-wide web content, services and applications (not least web-pages and web-based services);
- other internet applications such as email and 'voice over internet protocol' (such as *Skype* and other web-based telephone services).

All of these technologies are referred to throughout the education sector by a variety of terms – sometimes simply as 'computers', 'the internet' or digital technology. Many countries still talk of information technology (IT) to refer to computer-based systems, particularly software applications and computer hardware that can be used to produce, manipulate, store, communicate, and/or disseminate information. Some countries use terms like C&IT (communications and information technology). Yet in the UK the current favoured term for the use of digital technology in education is 'information and communications technology', or ICT for short.

The term 'ICT' came to prominence towards the mid-1990s as governments around the world began to recognize the need to highlight the potential of the internet. By this point many education technologists felt that 'IT' had become too closely aligned as a term with the specific use of computers, and a string of relatively unsuccessful applications such as video discs, laser discs and miniature televisions. 'Information and communications technology' became the accepted term of reference in some countries for the use of networked computerized information technologies in education. In theory, the 'C' of ICT was intended to stress both the 'C' of communication and the 'C' of convergence. ICT was intended to be an updating of the idea of IT by highlighting the rapid convergence of technological applications such as computer hardware and software, digital broadcast technologies, and telecommunications technologies such as mobile phones, and the internet as well as electronic information resources such as the worldwide web and CD-ROMs.

'ICT' as a whole-school concern or separate subject?

The clarity of ICT as a term since the mid-1990s has been compromised slightly by its dual use in education. In the UK at least, ICT is used to refer to the digital technologies themselves, but also to the discrete curriculum subject. In the original version of the National Curriculum for primary schools, the use of computers was part of Design and Technology, before enjoying several years of growth and development as a subject under the label of 'Information Technology'. The change in 2000 to a curriculum subject called 'ICT' signalled a formal move towards a more inclusive way of working with technologies in schools, with subsequent schemes of work emphasizing a cross-curricular approach. In this book we are more interested in this wider sense of ICT as a tool used by pupils and teachers across all aspects of school life.

Of course, whether to focus on ICT as a discrete part of the school curriculum or else spread ICT across everything that goes on inside a school has been a long-standing source of disagreement in education circles. Both approaches can be said to have their merits. The 'subject approach', for example, can be seen to give pupils and teachers a sufficient amount of time and space to concentrate on developing ICT skills and understanding, free from the many other pressures of schooling. Yet we would argue that digital technologies are now so deeply woven throughout the lives of pupils, teachers and schools that it makes more sense to see ICT in 'holistic' terms of technology use throughout all of the whole school day and activities.

The priorities of ICT

Having set out our terms of reference, we can now go on to consider the problems and issues that this book sets out to tackle. In particular, there are a whole host of questions that arise as soon as ICTs are introduced into educational settings – not least *why* should ICT be used in primary education? Whereas it may appear odd to ask such a basic question, anyone seeking to eventually suggest ways that ICTs may be better used in schools would do well to first consider some of the guiding beliefs that surround technology and education. Indeed, it is often simply presumed in educational discussions that ICT is inherently 'a good thing' for schools. Yet a range of different agendas and interests lie behind this faith in technology – many of which go some way towards explaining the apparent 'failure' of ICTs to transform primary schools and schooling, despite very substantial investment and a central place in the primary curriculum.

The priority of keeping up with technology

One of the most straightforward reasons why primary schools are seen to need to use ICT is the simple priority of 'keeping up' with the rest of modern life. The rapid development of computer technology over the last fifty years is illustrated ably by what technologists know as 'Moore's law'. This rule-of-thumb describes the long-term exponential trend that the number of transistors that can be placed on an microchip more or less doubles approximately every 2 years. This increasing technical capacity is accompanied by a steady increase in the usefulness of digital technologies in most areas of society – especially in business, public administration, the media and entertainment industries, and the home. Many people therefore feel that schools are placed in a constant position of being 'behind the times' with regard to technology use in comparison to other sectors of society. This creates the need for schools to respond to technological advances – what Robert Boody called the priority of 'running just to keep in place'.[6]

The point here is not that primary schools have actively resisted using new technologies in comparison to other areas of society. Rather it is argued that technology development has failed to have the same impact in schools as elsewhere. Throughout the 1970s, 1980s and into the 1990s, primary schools witnessed successive waves of new technological developments associated with the microcomputer, the PC and world-wide web. In hindsight, however, many of these technologies could be said to have rather passed primary education by. At best, only a handful of ICT activities and applications could be said to have established a lasting presence in primary school life during those years. Often the most successful technologies have been 'add-ons' to the main classroom experience, such as word-processors and desktop publishing software, some painting and drawing packages and a variety of CD-based encyclopaedias, resources and teaching titles. Other ICT applications have established a foothold in schools where enthusiastic teachers were on hand to promote them. For example, the *Logo* programming language and the associated *Turtle Graphics* packages and Roamer robots were common features in many schools during the 1980s and 1990s. Simulation programs such as *Granny's Garden* and *The Crystal Castle* also had an enduring popularity throughout this time, when many other applications failed.

However, it was not until the mainstream emergence of the internet in the mid-1990s that the primary sector was forced to respond on a widespread basis to the technological imperative of the 'information superhighway' and 'cyberspace'. In this sense, the growing significance of websites and email, alongside the increasing portability of laptop computers and mobile telephones, contributed to a boom in primary ICT during the 1990s and into the 2000s. Of course, the ICTs of the mid-1990s bear little relation to the ICTs of today. Just as the notion of 'IT' was felt to be nearing the end of its usefulness as a term in the mid-1990s, as we now move into the 2010s the notion of 'ICT' could be said to be looking equally outmoded in light of recent changes in the worldwide web – in particular, the emerging potential of 'web 2.0' technologies and the 'social' internet. Primary schools currently face a fresh set of technological developments to 'keep up with', based around an array of personalized and portable devices, as well as a new wave of web tools, applications and services. Particularly important is the requirement to develop online learning environments which mirror the real-life teaching and learning activities on an 'always-on' basis.

Table 1.1 Web 2.0 applications

Web 2.0 genre	Description	Popular examples
Social networking	Sites where online communities of users maintain 'profiles' of personal information and interact with each other.	*MySpace, Facebook*
Wikis	Web pages that any user with access can contribute new content, to or modify existing content.	*Wikipedia, Wiki-answers*
Virtual worlds	Virtual environments that users can explore as a character of their choice, meeting other users and competing in mini-games and themed tasks.	*Second Life, Free Realms*
Blogging	Websites where the author 'posts' regular entries of commentary, descriptions of events, pictures and so on. 'Micro-blogging' involves the posting of very short text entries – often in real time.	*Edublogs, Twitter*
Multiplayer online gaming	Online games where a large number of players interact with one another within a virtual environment. Games often involve role-playing, combat and 'quests'.	*RuneScape, World of Warcraft*
Folksonomy/ social tagging	The collaborative labelling and categorizing of online content by a group of users.	*Delicious, Digg*

Perhaps the most prominent current technological priority is that of 'web 2.0'. Alongside other labels such as the 'social web' and 'social software', the notion of 'web 2.0' provides a convenient umbrella term for a host of recent internet tools and practices. (see Table 1.1). Although differing in form and function, all these applications support online interaction between groups of users. 'Web 2.0' therefore refers to a recent mass socialization of internet connectivity that is centred on the collective actions of online user communities rather than individual users. These qualities are soon apparent if one contrasts the defining characteristics of popular web 2.0 applications with their earlier 'web 1.0' equivalents. For example, *Wikipedia* is distinct from the *Encyclopaedia Britannica Online* in that it is an open document that is created, updated, edited and refereed by its readers. *Wikipedia* is seen to derive accuracy and authority from ongoing group discussion and consensus rather than the word of one expert – what some people see as 'the wisdom of crowds'.[7]

It should be easy to see why web 2.0 is felt to be a priority for primary education. In contrast to the 'broadcast' mode of information exchange that characterized internet use in the 1990s, the web applications of today are seen to rely on information that is shared 'many-to-many' rather than being transmitted from 'one-to-many'. The success of web 2.0 applications is based around the making and sharing of content amongst communities of users, resulting in various forms of user-driven communication, collaboration and content creation and re-creation. Making things, sharing, commentating and working in groups are all activities that are supposed to lie at the heart of primary education. Thus web 2.0 tools now form the latest technological trend to which primary schools are under pressure to adapt.

The priority of keeping up with children

As the recent rise of the web 2.0 phase of internet use demonstrates, it often feels like the pace of ICT development prevents schools and teachers from taking stock or even making the most of what they know. Whether they like it or not, educators are faced with a constantly changing technological world that many people expect to be reflected in what schools do, and how they do it. These expectations come from adults and children alike – not least the generation of pupils who are now entering primary schools having been born into the twenty-first century not knowing a life without the internet and the mobile telephone. For many commentators these children are seen as so-called 'digital natives' who demand that their school experience matches the rest of their technology-saturated lifestyles.

The origins of the 'digital native' label go back to a series of articles written during the 2000s by the US technologist Marc Prensky. Since 2001, Prensky has detailed the generations of young people born since 1980 as 'digital natives' – describing what he sees as their innate confidence in using new technologies such as the internet, video games, mobile telephony and 'all the other toys and tools of the digital age'.[8] Rather than merely using digital technology as part of their everyday lives, Prensky argues that technology is now essential to children's everyday lives. He describes children as being 'immersed' and constantly 'sur-rounded' by these new technologies in ways that older generations are not. Recently, Prensky has argued that this almost permanent state of technological immersion and dependence can be seen in the lifestyles of a current generation of 'i-kids' who remain 'plugged into' portable, personalized devices such as mobile telephones, MP3 players and handheld games consoles.

This idea of the 'digital native' is based upon the common perception that present cohorts of children and young people have distinct characteristics that set them apart from their elders. In reference to post-baby boomer depictions of 'generation X' and 'generation Y', the children and young people of the early twenty-first century are often portrayed as 'generation M' (media), 'generation V' (virtual) or 'generation C' (referring to character-istics such as connected, creative and click).[9] These accounts all highlight what is seen as children's innate affinity with digital technologies. This natural inclination can be seen in recent scientific assertions that 'young people are hardwired' to use new forms of digital technology.[10] Similarly, Prensky talks of children now being 'fluent in the digital language of computers, video games and the internet'.[11]

Prensky is not the only author to note a generational shift. Don Tapscott has also spent much time detailing the high-tech activities and expectations of the 'net generation' of young people who 'grew up bathed in bits'.[12] Other commentators now talk of the 'born digital', 'homo zappiens', or 'net savvy' youth.[13] In a domestic sense these are children who are described as living 'digital childhoods' within 'media families'. From an educational viewpoint, these are the 'new millennial learners'.[14] All told, many popular and academic commentators recognize a distinct step-change in the ways in which modern forms of childhood and adolescence are steeped in the use of digital technology and media. Schools, it therefore follows, are faced with the priority of keeping up with these children and providing schooling that fits with their high-tech lives.

The priority of public expectation

Of course, much of the imperative for change stems from adult rather than child concerns. There is a general sense from employers, for example, that encouraging school children to use technology will be of long-term economic benefit in a world where future workforces are increasingly expected to make use of technology in all professions and walks of life. In this sense, as Sarah Holloway and Gill Valentine have observed, even primary schools are seen as 'places where children as workers of the future are educated'.[15] While it may not appear of immediate relevance to classroom teachers, this economic priority is perhaps the justification that is used most often for increasing the use of ICT in schools. As the Chief Inspector of Schools in England recently reasoned: 'ICT needs to be given high status, both by the government and in individual schools, in line with its importance to young people's future economic well-being.'[16]

Aside from these matters of economic success and 'employability', many adults also consider the ability to use ICTs to be an essential life-skill for primary-age children as they grow up into an 'information society'. Now most aspects of life in developed countries such as the UK are based increasingly around the use of ICT in one form or another – from shopping, leisure and entertainment to interacting with public and civic services. From this perspective there is a strong social imperative for schools to be introducing children to technology.

Whilst giving children the required skills to live and work in the modern world is important, the prioritization of increased ICT use in schools also comes from the personal beliefs and experiences of parents and teachers themselves. Many teachers and parents make extensive use of ICTs such as the internet and mobile phones in their 'real lives'. Buying consumer goods, researching holidays, pursuing hobbies and interests are all now common activities for many adults. Many parents work extensively with ICT and are therefore keen to see their children experience similar benefits at school. Moreover, many teachers and parents of primary-age children were themselves the recipients of ICT-based schooling as pupils throughout the 1980s and 1990s.

All of these personal experiences add up to the almost unconscious connection in the minds of many parents and guardians between ICT and the 'quality' of their child's education. Parents and grandparents will often purchase computer equipment for children in the hope that it will assist them with their homework and other 'worthy' informal learning activities – much as previous generations of parents would have purchased sets of encyclopaedias or employed home tutors. There is a booming market in home 'edutainment' products and online services, as parents look to boost their children's educational attainment and future job prospects by any means possible. In all these ways many parents see ICT as a desirable and 'pro-social' form of engagement with new media and technology.

It is understandable, then, that all of these expectations from the home will spill over into public opinions of what schools 'should be doing'. Many parents will expect to see a school boast the latest technology equipment as a symbol of its high quality of teaching and learning. Often the first thing that parents will want to see when looking around a school is the computer room or ICT suite. Growing numbers of parents also expect to be able to keep in contact with their child's school via email, websites, text messaging and so on. Making extensive and efficient use of ICT is therefore an important factor in many parents' views of what makes a 'good school'.

The priority of education policy

A final important driving force behind the prioritization of ICT in primary schools has undoubtedly been the requirements and expectations of education policy. The last fifteen years have seen ICTs become a prominent feature of education systems in most countries around the world. Nearly every developed country (and indeed many a developing country) now has a detailed 'educational ICT strategy' based around the broad aim of getting schools to use ICT in their teaching and learning. These strategies and initiatives most commonly involve spending significant amounts of money on computer hardware and internet connectivity, so that the internet is available in every classroom and there are sufficient computers for pupils and teachers to use. Much effort is also put into the training of teachers and the adjustment of the school curriculum to include ICT components. From Ethiopia's 'ICT in Education Implementation Strategy' to Estonia's 'Learning Tiger Programme', ICT forms a central part of the improvement and modernization of education systems around the world.

These political pressures to use ICT should not be under-estimated – especially in the UK. Indeed, alongside countries such as the USA, Singapore and South Korea, the UK is generally considered to have one of the most successful education ICT policy programmes in the world. Since 1997 the UK government is reckoned to have spent nearly £6 billion on ICT in schools through a sustained agenda of education technology policy-making. Most notably, the UK schools sector was subject to three distinct phases of policy-making over the 1998–2010 period. These include the 'National Grid for Learning' initiative and associated National Lottery funded teacher training programme between 1998 and 2002; the 'ICT in Schools' drive and associated Curriculum Online and e-learning credit schemes between 2002 and 2005; and the 'Harnessing Technology' agenda underpinned by the Department for Children, Schools and Families' 'e-learning strategy' between 2005 and 2010. Over the years, these flagship initiatives have been complemented by a succession of smaller programmes and schemes – from the provision of laptop computers for head teachers to the establishment of online content watchdogs. ICTs also formed a central element of the 'Building Schools for the Future' initiative that dedicated £45 billion to re-equipping all secondary schools in the UK.

Unlike similar policies in the 1980s and 1990s, one of the key features of these national ICT policy drives is that they are now directed at learners of all ages. In this sense primary and pre-school education has been as much the subject of these changes throughout the 2000s as secondary and tertiary sectors. As we enter the 2010s, ICT is as much a primary school issue as it is an issue for secondary schools or universities. For example, primary ICT is a key component of Singapore's ten-year master plan, 'Intelligent Nation 2015'. The current New Zealand 'Digital Strategy' has an explicit focus on primary ICT – seeking to use 'ICT meaningfully in early childhood education services to help children grow up as competent and confident learners and communicators'.[17] Similarly, the Australian government's Digital Education Revolution strategy supports the development of fibre broadband connections to all Australian primary schools, and providing online curriculum tools and resources to all students and teachers. Most European countries have also similar plans for the development of primary ICT – from the French Digital Strategy to the extensive Austrian Future Learning strategy based around the use of wikis, blogging and e-portfolios.

In England and Wales the current Harnessing Technology agenda has also set out a number of ambitious priorities for primary ICT. This agenda sets out the UK government's intention, amongst other things, to 'maximize investment' in schools' technology, develop an 'e-confident education and skills system', and ensure that all learners 'benefit' from ICT. Although it may be tempting to dismiss some of these aims as civil service jargon, the Harnessing Technology goals mark a significant step in school ICT use – not least in emphasizing the 'entitlement' of the individual learner in terms of their ICT use in school. This can be seen, for instance, in the wide range of qualities that pupils are now entitled to expect from their schools' ICT provision:

- personalized learning, reflecting learners' interests, preferred approaches, abilities and choices, and tailored access to materials and content;
- access to online support and tuition, alongside tailored personal support from trained advisers and other professionals;
- entitlement to tools to support learning, and support to become fluent and proficient in their use;
- integration of online learning with provision in school;
- the need for accessible online information, advice and guidance, raising aspirations, facilitating learning pathways, and enabling access to employment;
- access to continuing support to acquire and update skills, including support in using technology safely;
- appropriate methods and avenues for learner consultation and engagement.

KEY ISSUE

The place of ICT in the primary curriculum

IT and ICT have been a part of the National Curriculum for England and Wales since its inception in 1988. At the time of conducting the research for this book, 'ICT' was one of nine foundation subjects in the English Primary National Curriculum. In addition ICT was also described as a set of capabilities to be developed by the use of new technologies across all curriculum subjects. Similarly, in Scotland the area of 'technologies' was one of eight 'curriculum areas' within the Scottish Curriculum for Excellence. Curriculum orders such as these have shaped teachers' and learners' use of ICT in a number of ways – not least the need to see ICT as a shared responsibility across the school as well as a discrete subject area.

More recently a range of radical recommendations has been made for reforming the primary curriculum in line with the needs of the twenty-first century. A large UK government enquiry (the Rose Report) and an independent Cambridge Primary Review both recommended substantial changes to what is taught in primary schools, how learning is managed and how it is assessed. The scope of these changes should not be underestimated, with the Rose Report in particular described as 'the most significant reform of timetables since the National Curriculum was introduced'.[18] The Rose Report placed ICT at the heart of its newly defined programmes of learning (of which more later) and continued the cross-curricular development of ICT. The diffusion of ICT into a range of other curriculum experiences and alignment with much wider life-skills was signalled in the requirement for primary schools to:

> strengthen the teaching and learning of ICT to enable children to be independent and confident users of technology by the end of primary education. Used well, technology strongly develops the study and learning skills children need now and in the future, including the fundamentals of 'e-safety'. Embedding ICT throughout the primary curriculum and giving it greater prominence within the core of 'Essentials for Learning and Life' will provide children with more opportunities to harness the potential of technology to enhance learning.[19]

ICT was also a prominent concern of the Cambridge Primary Review, which highlighted concerns over whether the 'importance' of ICT currently 'was properly reflected in the curriculum'.[20] In particular, the Cambridge Review highlighted the need to resolve the debate over whether ICT should be a subject area in its right, or else a cross-curricular skill. As the authors of the review remarked, a strong belief persists within the education technology community:

that ICT was of sufficient importance and complexity to be handled as a stand-alone subject, like mathematics. Many teachers and teacher trainers, on the other hand, viewed it more as a resource, for example for children's writing ... The division between those who regarded ICT as a cross-curricular tool or skill and those who believed it should be timetabled as a subject in its own right was marked.[21]

The final recommendations of these reviews regarding ICT made interesting reading. The Cambridge Primary Review simply recommended a spreading of ICT across the curriculum, with an emphasis put on pupils 'doing' ICT in the form of 'the electronic handling of information through ICT' complemented by the development of an 'understanding' of the actions and consequences of technology use.[22] The Rose Report also made a number of detailed and more specific recommendations about ICT. In particular, it was suggested that the level of lessons in ICT in primary schools should be raised to the current levels of secondary school teaching. In this sense, one of the key outcomes of the Rose recommendations was a sense that primary ICT should play a key role in 'freeing up' secondary school ICT by making sure that pupils are adequately trained in ICT skills during their primary education. As Sir James Rose put it, primary schools 'need to move with the times and teach ... secondary school ICT earlier at primary'.[23]

Primary schools in England therefore face a changing use of ICT as the 2010s progress. Under the core curriculum area of 'scientific and technological understanding', the Rose Report argued that all children should leave primary schools familiar with the internet as a source of information and as a means of communication. As well as developing 'fluency' in keyboard skills, spellchecker and search engine use, the report highlighted the need to be familiar with new web 2.0 applications such as blogging, *Wikipedia*, podcasting and *Twitter* – making the most of the computer 'know-how' that children already possess by the time they reach school. A number of suggestions have since been given of how ICT could be used to enhance primary teaching. Recommendations have been made, for example, for the use of *Google* Earth in geography, using spreadsheets to calculate budgets in maths, and even using video conferencing to learn languages from schools elsewhere in the world. Significantly, in the newly defined version of literacy, the production of 'multimodal' texts is included alongside print forms – perhaps signalling a formal media literacy requirement in the new curriculum and placing ICTs in another core curriculum area.

While the finer details of these recommendations will be debated and argued over as the new primary curriculum takes shape in schools, one thing remains certain – ICT is set to become an even more significant and perhaps even more prominent part of the primary curriculum than ever before.

The pressures of primary ICT

From these brief descriptions alone, we can see why ICT is considered to be an important priority for primary education, as well as being a site of intense debate in schools and elsewhere. Of course, we should not get too carried away with the overriding importance of ICT. Primary schools face many priorities other than ICT – such as special educational needs, literacy, numeracy, bullying and so on. Many teachers and parents also hold equally as strong views on the need to keep primary education as a free, fun and unfettered space for young children to develop socially, emotionally and intellectually. Yet amidst these other concerns, the need to be making extensive use of ICTs in all aspects of school life remains a constant, underlying issue for primary teachers and leaders.

All of these priorities and expectations leave primary schools and teachers under considerable pressure to make 'good' use of ICTs. Whilst few people would argue against this sentiment in principle, in practice what is meant by 'good' covers a range of agendas that are often not concerned directly with classroom teaching or pupil learning. This leaves ICT use pulled in a number of different directions by a number of different interests. In particular, teachers are left in the unenviable position of having to fulfil a number of briefs when it comes to using ICT. If we are to reach realistic suggestions for changing ICT practice it is important that we are aware of the wider pressures and agendas that underlie primary ICT.

The pressures for 'effective' use of ICT

As most readers will already be aware, primary ICT fulfils a number of priorities that are not related directly to pupil learning. This is perhaps most obvious from a governmental point of view. If we reconsider the 'Harnessing Technology' agenda outlined earlier in this chapter, we can see a number of significant exhortative words and phrases associated with what schools should be doing with ICT. Teachers and schools are urged, for example, to concentrate on 'maximizing investment' in technology, developing an 'e-confident education and skills system', and ensuring that all learners 'benefit' from ICT. In a similar manner, government ministers talk keenly of encouraging schools to make 'proper', 'appropriate' and 'consistent' use of technology.[24] The government's education ICT agency, Becta, also often talks of schools making 'effective' use of ICT to 'support effective' learning, teaching and administration.

All these words and phrases should not be dismissed as fuzzy and vague political sloganeering and sound bites. Instead they highlight the wide remit of schools' ICT use. From the point of view of governments and policy-makers such words and phrases can be seen to relate to at least three different aspects of ICT use in schools, namely:

- using ICTs to enhance the quality of teaching and learning – especially in relation to what policy-makers term educational 'standards and attainment';
- using ICTs to increase the organizational efficiency of schools – especially in terms of bureaucratic and administrative processes;
- using ICTs to develop skills relevant to the needs of the economy.

These are substantial issues that are not necessarily foremost in most teachers' minds when deciding whether or not to use ICT in their teaching. Yet it is important to recognize that much of the urgency and 'need' to make more use of ICT in primary education is related directly to these concerns. In this sense we need to remain aware in our later discussions that ICT in the primary classroom is being driven by much wider agendas relating to the 'transformation' of public sector services and national success in the global economy.

The pressures for 'engaging' use of ICT

Of course, not all of the pressures facing schools relate to matters of global economics and politics. As discussed earlier in this chapter, the changing technological backgrounds of children and young people are also seen to leave schools facing an increased demand for ICT use. There is a growing belief amongst many educationalists that technology-based learning is 'what children want'. This leaves schools and teachers under pressure to develop ways of working that are more aligned with a 'sense' of children's contemporary technology use and lifestyles. In terms of the emergence of web 2.0 technologies, for example, this is seen to include providing forms of learning that are based around play, expression, reflection, exploration and the creation rather than consumption of information and knowledge.

Making use of ICTs in ways that appeal to children's

technological interests and passions is seen to benefit schools in a number of ways – not least the increased engagement and motivation of learners. It is now being argued that ICTs offer teachers an opportunity to (re)connect with otherwise disaffected and disengaged learners. For example, web 2.0 tools and activities have been argued to be 'a massive part of what excites young people and therefore should contribute to [their] persistence and motivation to learn'.[25] ICT use is also being promoted as a ready means of fulfilling UK school inspection agencies' demands for teachers to produce lessons that are fun, entertaining and motivating.

These pressures are supported by some empirical evidence of the motivating nature of ICT-based teaching. For example, education researchers have noted the increased enjoyment, enthusiasm, stimulation and fun that pupils show when using ICT in class.[26] In a survey of 17 schools across England, Don Passey and colleagues identified a positive overall motivational impact of ICT, noting that pupils were more committed to learn and there was evidence that ICT impacted positively on pupils' attitudes towards and engagement with their school work.[27] The researchers also reported some evidence from pupils and school staff that behaviour in class was better when ICT was used. Interestingly, this study suggested that these motivational effects were stronger for primary schools than they were for secondary schools.

The pressures for 'safe' use of ICT

Besides making primary education more engaging and exciting for children and besides meeting the needs of organizational efficiency and the economy, a further pressure put upon ICT use in schools is that of ensuring the 'safety' of children when using technology. As we shall go on to discuss throughout this book, primary schools are being urged constantly by governments, parents and child experts to regulate and control children's contact with ICT. This is most commonly seen to involve the protection of children from the increased potential to be 'at risk' when using ICTs. These risks are especially seen to occur through 'inappropriate' and 'challenging' uses of the internet which place the child at risk of harming both themselves and others.

As Kay Withers outlines, a number of specific issues dominate debates on how schools should best protect children from the dangers posed by the internet.[28] These include:

- exposure to age-inappropriate content;
- exposure to violent content;
- exposure to sexual content;
- involvement in cyber-bullying;
- developing positive attitudes to safety;
- developing positive attitudes to privacy;
- exposure to advertising;
- plagiarism and the credibility of online information.

All of these concerns were recently brought into focus by the UK government's Byron Review.[29] This made a number of recommendations, including forming a UK Council on Child Internet Safety to improve industry regulation and provide better information and education via government, law enforcement, schools and children's services. Similar recommendations have been made in the US by the 'Internet Safety Technical Task Force' of the states' attorneys general.[30] In many countries, therefore, schools are faced with growing moral pressure to help children make safe and risk-free use of ICTs. Clearly this is a cultural as well as a technological issue that involves helping children see ICT differently and more critically.

Conclusions

This chapter has illustrated how and why ICT is now an important part of primary education. Above all, it has shown that a lot of the reasons for promoting ICT use in schools are not concerned directly with pupils and learning. Instead, many of the reasons why ICT now occupies such a prominent position in discussions about primary education are based around symbolic rather than practical concerns. Some of these concerns are related to the changing nature of modern life and society in an increasingly 'digital age' and with children's seemingly all-pervasive technology-based lifestyles. Other concerns are related with the future fortunes of national economies.

Even when the pressures to use ICT are school-related, these reasons are often unconnected to the immediate needs of teachers and pupils. Much of this chapter's discussion of ICT in primary education has shown the influence of the 'new managerialism' that has now crept into the running of even the smallest of primary schools. ICT use in schools is often justified in managerial terms of efficiency, effectiveness, modernization, rationalization and the ultimate reduction of spending costs. ICTs are now a key part of how schools have to become more 'entrepreneurial' in their approaches to dealing with the business of teaching and learning. There is now a growing belief that the 'smart school' is an ICT-using school. Indeed, ICTs have become a vital part of the market 'branding' of primary schools, bestowing a high-tech sheen on schools' often low-tech practices.

Although ICT is not the only area of primary education that is subject to these 'wider' influences and concerns, there is a danger that the symbolic and political aspects of primary ICT put undue pressure on teachers and learners and – ultimately – turn primary ICT in something of an unsolvable problem. We can already see, for example, how ICT has become something of a yardstick for efficiency, productivity and modernization. Concerns are being raised that ICT has now become part of what Stephen Ball terms 'the terrors of performativity' for teachers – where teaching is driven by responding to targets, indicators and evaluations, as opposed to what may be best for their pupils (or even what may be best for teachers).[31]

We therefore need to think carefully about how ICT can be moved away from these 'big' pressures and priorities, and towards the more immediate concerns, issues and pleasures that constitute the day-to-day experience of primary education 'at the chalk-face'. The next chapter in this book considers the promises and the problems facing individual learners, teachers and schools when it comes to using ICT in primary education. Above all, it is our intention for the rest of this book to try to ignore the 'big' priorities and pressures of ICT as much as possible. Unlike many other writers on schools and technology, it is our intention to think about the small-scale, localized impacts and aspects of ICT and schools. If we are looking to improve how ICTs are used in primary schools we should not be wasting too much of our time arguing for the fundamental change of the primary school system. The concerns and agendas of politicians, policy-makers, employers and parents – however misinformed – are unlikely to be easily swayed. Instead, we need to find ways of working around all the pressures and priorities usually associated with ICTs in schools. Our recommendations for improvement should be 'bottom-up' rather than 'top-down'.

In this sense we should try to step back from arguments over the relative merits of one technology over another, and unanswerable debates over whether ICT 'works' in education. There have been hundreds of books over the last thirty years that have described at length the 'potential' of educational ICTs and have explained why they *could* be good for primary pupils and teachers. We believe that the more important questions about primary ICT centre on how this undoubted potential is being worked out in practice and what – if anything – can be done to make things better in the immediate future. With these thoughts in mind, Chapter 2 now goes on to consider the promises of ICT for individual learners, and the problems that teachers and schools face as a result.

2 The promises and problems of primary ICT

Overview: This chapter starts by considering the educational potential of ICTs – in particular, the benefits they are seen to give to pupils. In contrast, we then highlight the 'digital disconnect' that many people believe is appearing between increasingly high-tech pupils and their rather more low-tech schools. We consider the growing belief that primary schools are simply unable to adapt to the demands of digital technology. In particular, we review some of the solutions currently suggested by educational technologists – most of which involve making sweeping long-term changes to the education system. We conclude that if primary ICT is to be improved in the short term, then realistic approaches are required that seek to make minor changes 'around the edges' of the primary school.

The promises of ICT for learners

Amidst the 'big' priorities and pressures outlined in Chapter 1, it is surprising that people often fail to give much thought to how individual learners are actually making use of ICTs. Of course ICTs offer many advantages to teachers, schools and even governments. But as the ultimate 'end-users' of technology-based learning, the most important elements of primary ICT are surely the pupils themselves. In this regard, it is worthwhile taking time to consider the many promises that ICTs offer to pupils – not least the promise of improving the ways that pupils learn, the promise of 'fitting' learning around the needs of the individual, and generally bringing schooling closer to the ways in which current generations of children live their lives outside school.

The ability of ICT to improve learning

Digital technologies are widely seen to support and often enhance children's capacity to process information and learn. Some authors claim that ICTs are a key part of modern-day children's capacity to 'think and process information fundamentally differently from their predecessors'.[1] Here it is argued that ICT use leads to children being able to learn at high speed, make random connections, process visual and dynamic information and learn through digitally-based play and interactions. Whilst far-fetched, the general essence of such claims is supported by some scientific evidence. A growing number of neuroscientific studies suggest, for example, that internet use can enhance children's capacity to develop greater working memory, be more adept at perceptual learning, and have better motor skills.[2]

Besides these neurological and cognitive advantages, ICT is also seen to have transformed the manner in which children are now able to learn. Children's ability to access vast digital networks of information, resources and people is seen to lead to learning in ways that are 'situated' within authentic contexts – helping children get to know things much quicker and in greater quantity than would ever have been possible before. As Marc Prensky speculates, 'within the working lives of our students, technology will become a billion times more powerful, likely more powerful than the human brain'.[3] In this sense, ICT is seen to have improved immeasurably what children can learn and how they can learn it, often in ways and places far removed from the concerns of traditional 'school' education.

All these descriptions of the 'better' and 'different' forms of learning that are associated with ICT use fit well with popular 'socio-cultural' theories of learning that emerged from the work of psychologists such as Lev Vygotsky during the twentieth century. Socio-cultural theories of learning see 'active' and 'authentic' learning as most likely to take place within groups of people and 'learning objects' where the construction of knowledge by learners can be nurtured and supported in a community environment. Indeed, much of the learning potential of ICTs is seen to derive from learners' own construction of knowledge. As we saw in Chapter 1, a sense of 'learning by doing' and by 'making things' underpins the enthusiasm amongst many experts for the educational potential of the participative learning cultures of web 2.0 applications such as virtual worlds and multi-player online games. Similarly, the ability to collaboratively edit as well as individually read resources such as *Wikipedia* is seen to lead young people to learn in powerful groups. As the creator of *Wikipedia* has argued, children can use such applications to learn 'what works and what does not in a way that was not possible with books. You wouldn't have even joined the debate.'[4]

Many of these new and better forms of learning are based upon giving children increased access to 'informal learning' opportunities. The notion of informal learning can be described most accurately as learning that takes place outside the control of the formal education system. Informal learning includes often unintentional learning that is stimulated by general interests – learning which is 'caught not taught'.[5] Digital technologies such as the

---

KEY ISSUE

Proving the 'effect' of ICT on learning

With so much money being spent on ICT in schools, pinpointing the 'effect' or 'impact' of ICT use on children's learning has become one of the main 'holy grails' of education technology research. Although there is much anecdotal and case study evidence from classrooms around the world that ICT can be used to support and enhance learning, there is very little rigorous evidence of the educational impact of ICT use on a wide-spread scale. Despite the difficulty of identifying tangible gains, there is still a strong belief amongst many policy-makers and educationalists that ICT 'works' in education. The UK government, for example, continues to make assurances that 'we know from the research evidence the difference that information technology can make.'[6]

Although many people have looked at district-wide and national statistics for a relationship between measures of learning and ICT investment and use, the evidence remains inconclusive. Although some studies report moderate gains, other studies report no noticeable difference.[7] This lack of effectiveness was illustrated in the 2000s when a number of experimental studies and economic analyses in US, Israeli, German and Dutch high schools all reported non-existent or even negative correlations between levels of ICT use and eventual learning outcomes.[8]

Many educationalists are now coming to the conclusion that it is perhaps unwise to try to disentangle the 'effect' of ICT use amidst all the other factors and changes taking place in schooling. Schools and classrooms are simply not good settings for the sort of experimental research that can 'prove' that one thing 'causes' something else to happen. With so many initiatives and investments taking place in schools it is virtually impossible to pinpoint any specific 'effect' of ICT on learning. In this sense, learning gains in a technology-rich classroom could be said to be due to a combination of all these factors – not least a particularly good teacher or group of pupils.

internet and mobile telephones are seen as especially conducive to informal learning given their enhanced connections between people, places, products and services – allowing new opportunities for informal exchange of expertise, knowledge and folk-wisdom.

The ability of ICT to help learning fit better with learners' ways of life

As these descriptions suggest, one of the main educational benefits of ICT is the ability to put the learner at the centre of any learning event or activity. Besides the cognitive benefits of doing so, this is seen to be a very important way of helping learning 'fit' better with current generations of children who are now used to lifestyles outside school that are increasingly 'individualized' and 'persona-lized'. This increased personalization of everyday life is seen to increase children's autonomy over the nature and form of what they do, as well as where, when and how they do it. In this sense, children are seen to be increasingly accustomed to a 'personalized' tailoring of activities and services that they are unlikely to find in a traditional school set-up.

ICT use is therefore seen as an appropriate means of making what goes on inside schools more relevant and appropriate to the lives of 'digital natives'. As we saw in Chapter 1, current generations of primary pupils are seen to have much faster and flexible lifestyles than previous generations. It is argued that ICTs have helped children and young people be part of a 'multitasking generation', reliant on a 'digital juggling' of their daily activities and commitments.[9] Making more use of ICTs is therefore seen to help schools evolve from being passive deliverers of educational instruction and custodians of knowledge. Instead children are allowed a more active role in choosing the nature, place, pace and timing of their learning.

Web 2.0 technologies, in particular, are seen as a ready way of increasing the 'goodness of fit' between what children are used to doing outside school, and what they are expected to do inside school. Much has been written, for example, about how children are now immersed in rich 'communities of practice' supported by internet applications such as social networking sites, wikis and virtual worlds. Children are therefore seen as a 'collaboration generation',[10] eager to work together towards common goals, share content and draw upon 'the power of mass collaboration'.[11] Web 2.0 technologies are also argued to have made children used to more open and 'fairer' ways of doing things, where anyone can do anything whenever they want. As Gwen Solomon and Lynne Schrum conclude, 'everyone can participate thanks to social networking and collaborative tools and the abundance of web 2.0 sites … The web is no longer a one-way street where someone controls the content. Anyone can control content in a web 2.0 world.'[12] Making use of these technologies in schools is seen as an obvious way to make schools more relevant and fairer places for children to learn.

KEY ISSUE

Arguments against the use of ICT in education

Although the use of ICTs in education is usually presented in a positive light, some people remain opposed to the increased use of technology in the classroom. As the internet has developed as a mainstream activity, a number of educational commentators have begun to point to a range of disadvantages and dangers of encouraging technology use in the classroom.

For instance, concerns persist over an intellectual 'dumbing down' associated with using ICTs to access information and knowledge. Some critics argue that excessive use of the internet is now hampering many children's ability to gather information in a discerning manner. As Andrew Keen puts it, current generations of school children are often 'taking search-engine results as gospel.'[13] Children are argued to have little awareness of notions of the authorship, authenticity or authority of a piece of information. Keen talks of fostering a 'younger generation of intellectual kleptomaniacs, who think their ability to cut and paste a well-phrased thought or opinion makes it their own.'[14]

The lack of face-to-face interaction associated with ICT use has also prompted fears over imminent declines in children's cognitive skills, as well as the unbalancing of their hormone levels and declines in mental performance.[15] Susan Greenfield, professor of synaptic pharmacology at the University of Oxford, is one such critic. Greenfield has recently argued, for example, that social networking sites are linked to the rise of attention-deficit disorder amongst children, increased levels of autism as well as decreased ability to empathize and be social with other people. According to Greenfield, children's experiences of social networking sites and other web 2.0 tools

are devoid of cohesive narrative and long-term significance. As a consequence, the mid-21st century mind might almost be infantilised, characterised by short attention spans, sensationalism, inability to empathise and a shaky sense of identity ... It is hard to see how living this way on a daily basis will not result in brains, or rather minds, different from those of previous generations.[16]

Aside from the detrimental effect on 'traditional' skills and literacies, concerns have also been raised that digital technologies may be contributing to an increased disaffection and 'alienation' of children from schools and classroom learning. For example, current cohorts of school pupils have been described as being more interested in using digital technologies such as the internet or mobile telephony for self-expression and self-promotion than for actually listening to and learning from others. These concerns have prompted some commentators to point to the digital acceleration of 'a culture of disrespect' between students and their schools and teachers.[17]

Whether one agrees with these arguments or not, they appear to be taken seriously by those in power, with all manner of official organizations and bodies beginning to express such concerns. The UK Secretary of State for Education has warned teachers against 'the sinister downside of modern technology'.[18] Susan Greenfield's comments about social networking were part of a formal debate in the House of Lords. Even organizations such as the Catholic Church have begun to add their voice against ICT. Pope Benedict XVI has, for example, been known to make links between excessive computer use and social isolation and depression. Other members of the clergy have also called for young Catholics to abstain from internet use for Lent – to 'cleanse themselves from the virtual world and get back in touch with themselves', as the Archbishop of Modena put it.[19]

The growing problems of ICT for schools

These promises of ICT are all very well in theory, but many readers will struggle to see how the types of ICT use outlined above could fit easily with the day-to-day realities of primary schooling. As with all aspects of education and technology, it is important to remember that all of the promises and descriptions of ICT use covered in this chapter so far are based upon an ideal 'best case scenario'. As such it is perhaps not surprising that the realities of ICT use in primary education often fall well short of these potential benefits. Although this may not a surprise for most readers, many education commentators still forget to consider the 'messy realities' of primary schools and classrooms when enthusing about the latest 'next big thing' in education technology. With this need for realism in mind, it is perhaps time for us to move on from the promises of ICT in an ideal world, and consider what we know about schools' use of ICT in practice.

At first glance, ICTs appear to be used with great success within primary schools. In the UK, for example, the substantial increases in funding, resourcing and support of primary ICT deriving from the government's ICT in Schools strategy during the 2000s appear to have greatly reduced many of the barriers to ICT use in UK primary education that were in existence during the 1980s and 1990s. The issue of adequate resourcing is now far less of a problem than it was before. It is reckoned that the UK primary sector now spends annually over £300 million on ICT hardware and infrastructure, as well as an additional £80 million on software and content. These figures equate to the typical primary school having an annual ICT budget of nearly £16,000.

As a result of all this spending, the ratio of pupils to computers in primary schools has diminished from 107 pupils per computer in 1985 to around 7 in 2008.[20] Most classrooms are now equipped with interactive whiteboards, and primary teachers are reported to be more technically confident and more likely to make regular use of ICT in their teaching than their secondary school counterparts.[21] With ICT use now an embedded cross-curricular priority in primary schools, concerns over lack of access and expertise are felt to be less applicable than in the 1980s and 1990s. Indeed, the last decade has certainly seen the enhancement of 'the UK's leading reputation' for ICT in primary education.[22]

Yet whilst examples of best practice with ICT can be found throughout the primary school system, on the whole it should be admitted that ICT use is far from perfect. This was illustrated in Becta's admission in 2007 that 'only one in six schools and colleges are getting the full benefit of using technology in a truly effective way'.[23] This stark statement recognized that although the vast majority of primary pupils now make some use of ICTs in school, patterns of sustained and varied engagement with technology continue to differ between and within schools. Even within the same local authority or school district, wide gaps will be apparent between the most innovative and successful schools and those barely using ICT. In particular, issues of technical difficulties and variations in access continue to be reported as impinging on the effectiveness of all classroom use of ICT resources such as computers, the internet and interactive whiteboards.[24] Although most schools are now purchasing substantial amounts of ICT equipment and resources, there is often a lack of long-term support 'on the ground' for teachers with respect to technical support or the realistic integration of ICT into the curriculum.

Furthermore, in contrast to the promises of collaboration and sharing of knowledge outlined earlier, concerns remain that in-school uses of new technologies remain dominated by the delivery of information through interactive whiteboards, and the 'cutting and pasting' of online material retrieved from search engines such as *Google* into text documents and *PowerPoint* presentations. Pupil and teacher use of the internet is often reported to be limited by a range of filtering, firewalls and other blocking procedures, such as the withholding of administrator rights on local machines. The limitations of school building design and amount of available space are also reported as limiting ICT use. Equipment failure blights the daily experience of many teachers, together with the difficulty of even undertaking the simplest task such as downloading a small video clip for sharing with pupils.

All of these issues contribute to the growing complaint that schools' ICT use continues to be far too formal and constrained in nature – especially when compared to children's rather more expansive engagement with digital media outside the classroom. In-school ICT use has been characterized by some critics as rule-governed behaviour – something that is done *to* rather than done *by* pupils. This has led to perhaps the most damning conclusion of all, that school use of ICT is inauthentic, forced and 'pretend'. As the Australian commentator Chris Bigum concluded:

> Unlike other spheres of human work in which these technologies are deployed to solve actual problems or re-engineer practices, in education the task is almost always to find useful things to do with the technology. The consequence is that classroom practices typically remain pretend and fabricated. Because the work is chiefly concerned with fitting into the classroom or curriculum logic, scant attention is paid to uses to which the technology is being put beyond the classroom. Computing and communication technologies use in the classroom is therefore almost automatically positioned as inauthentic or, at best, only having meaning in the isolated and largely self-contained sphere in which educational applications of these technologies are discussed and debated.[25]

The growing digital disconnection between primary schools and their pupils

Although Bigum's view may appear a little alarmist, it illustrates the seriousness of the so-called 'digital dilemma' that many education commentators now see schools facing as the twenty-first century draws on. It is being argued, for example, that a revitalization of schools' ICT use is essential if schools are not to experience 'a legitimacy crisis with kids'.[26] Some researchers are issuing stark warnings of a new ICT-driven 'generation gap' and growing 'digital disconnect' appearing between learners accustomed to high levels of ICT use in all aspects of their everyday lives except school.[27] In this sense it is feared that current generations of technology-savvy children will become 'aliens' in their own classrooms and may become disaffected and questioning of their wider educational experiences.[28]

Many people see this increasing gulf as rooted in the growing generation gap between the adult world of education and today's cohorts of children. Indeed, the idea of 'digital natives' outlined in Chapter 1 implies a distinct disjuncture between children and older generations. Marc Prensky described all adults born before 1980 as 'digital immigrants' who have been forced to adapt to a world of digital media after years of leading 'pre-digital' lifestyles. In this sense many adults are felt to lack the technological fluency of younger generations and find the skills possessed by them unfamiliar and often foreign.[29] As Marc Prensky concludes:

> I refer to those of us who were not born into the digital world as 'digital immigrants'. We have adopted many aspects of the technology, but just like those who learn another language later in life, we retain an 'accent' because we still have one foot in the past. We will read a manual, for example, to understand a program before we think to let the program teach itself. Our accent from the pre-digital world often makes it difficult for us to effectively communicate with our students.[30]

This argument is seen to be especially applicable to schools and schooling. All told, the emerging received wisdom amongst many educationalists and technologists is that almost every aspect of schools and those within them lacks what it takes, as Roger Dale and Susan Robertson have put it, to 'go with the technological flow'.[31] For instance, school buildings are criticized as being architecturally unsuitable for widespread networked and wireless technology use. Teachers are seen to be too old, incompetent or uninterested to integrate ICT into their teaching. School leaders and administrators are seen to lack the required direction or foresight to make the most of the increased levels of funding coming their way. School curricula are seen to remain too rigid and entrenched in pre-digital ways of thinking. Put simply, there is a growing sense that schools simply 'don't get' modern technologies and the children that use them.

Current visions of change

Of course, these portrayals of digital natives and immigrants are based upon deliberately exaggerated caricatures of today's children and adults. Yet behind the polemic of the digital native debate, these arguments do highlight a distinct difference between the educational potential of ICTs and the realities of ICT use in many schools. Although varying in the severity of their diagnosis, there is a clear consensus amongst education and technology commentators that primary schools 'could do better' when it comes to ICT. Of course, some people assume that such improvements will be inevitable as schools are forced to change over time due to the sheer weight of expectation from up-coming generations of learners and teachers as well as by curriculum reform. Nevertheless, growing numbers of people are beginning to lose patience with this 'diffusion' approach and argue instead that some form of substantial alteration is required to the organization of primary education. In this spirit, a number of radical 'solutions' are currently being suggested for the technology-led reformation of schools. These range from proposals that schools should be completely reorganized along technological lines, to the idea that schools should be established as technology-free zones. The idea of getting rid of schools altogether is also being taken very seriously. Before we can consider some slightly less extreme suggestions for change, it is worth giving a little thought as to why many people feel so strongly about making such drastic changes.

Using schools to shut down ICT

Some people believe firmly that schools should maintain – and even strengthen – their disconnection from technology. Here, it is argued that schools should be recognized as different and distinct from the rest of children's 'real lives', and that few concessions should be made to accommodating technology-supported ways of doing things. Teachers' and schools' main concern with ICT should be with enforcing the regulation and control of young people's engagement with technology. These responses should focus on protecting children from the emotional and intellectual 'risks' seen to arise from excessive digital technology use.

These ideas are apparent, for example, in suggestions that schools should be used as sites to protect children from their digital excesses. Andrew Keen, for example, argues for the increased filtering and blocking of internet content in schools, reasoning that 'educators simply can't monitor what the kids are looking at all the time'.[32] A growing number of commentators are reaching the conclusion that schools should be constructed as sites where the tendency towards excessive ICT use amongst many children should be tempered and checked. It is argued that teachers and schools should work towards a 'de-powering' rather than an empowering of the digital native.

Some commentators have gone so far as to suggest that schools could actively establish themselves as ICT-free zones. Instead of grappling with new ways of technology-based learning, schools should deliberately concentrate on traditional teaching. In this sense schools should be encouraged to use top-down, instructive ways of teaching, based around a set curriculum and a rigid timetable. This approach acknowledges that a lot of learning is hard work rather than 'fun' and 'play', and that children often learn best by being told by a teacher rather than finding out for themselves. In this way the school could function as a 'fortress' of quality learning. As Stephen Heppell and colleagues contended:

> the 'Fortress School' embraces the school as the single validator of learning for the community with an almost monastic view of the school's role and function. The reification, deification even, of 'legitimate' learning would also lend itself philosophically to mechanistic individualised learning 'cells' and 'delivery' based learning systems, to a lack of debate or choice about what is to be learned ... Arguably, for many tough communities the fortress school offers a focus for ambition and even a beacon of hope.[33]

Using ICT to shut down the school

The idea of the 'fortress school' stands in stark contrast to the increasingly popular idea that technology-based learning should replace the idea of school altogether. Growing numbers of educationalists are concluding that the school is a 'dead' site for technology use and perhaps will never be able to adapt sufficiently to the challenge and disruption of the computer, internet and other digital technologies. In this sense the school should be seen as an outmoded technology from a past industrial age that is in need of being dismantled. Trying to integrate ICTs into schools has been compared to 'trying to put an internal combustion engine in a horse'.[34] Some highly esteemed computer scientists and 'learning technologists' have therefore talked of the technology-led 'blowing-up' of the conventional school.[35]

This turn away from the school as a viable site of ICT use is apparent across the academic education technology community. Authors such as Seymour Papert have long promoted arguments that schools and schooling are 'are relics from an earlier period of knowledge technology'[36] and that new technology will 'over-throw the accepted structure of school, the idea of curriculum, the segregation of children by age and pretty well everything that the education establishment will defend to the bitter end'.[37] Similar sentiments are now apparent elsewhere – such as the sociologist Manuel Castells' assertion that 'education is the most conservative system as to changing anything since the middle ages', making the 'rules, the format, the organisation of schools ... completely different' from other areas of the modern information age.[38]

Powerful arguments such as these continue to be put forward – reasoning that children are better off learning amongst themselves through ICT. Some technologists such as Nicholas Negroponte contend that children should be allowed to gain an education through the 'hard fun' of creating and playing in virtual worlds rather than being subjected to the 'teaching disabled' pedagogies of the conventional classroom.[39] In particular, internet technologies are felt to provide children with a ready means to circumvent the traditional structures of their schools and access the learning opportunities that their 'schools are not providing', as Henry Jenkins has put it.[40] For example, web 2.0 tools such as wikis, social networking and folksonomy software are seen to be able to move education away from being 'a special activity that takes place in special places at special times, in which children are instructed in subjects for reasons they little understand'.[41] Instead, ICTs are able to make education a 'fluid' arrangement where learning can involve a variety of people and places throughout a community for a variety of reasons. In this respect, much faith continues to be vested in digital technologies as a catalyst for the total substitution of the 'old fashioned' modes of teaching, learning and schooling.

Using ICT to reinvent the school

Although the latter arguments are taken very seriously by some very influential people in education, most readers would see them as rather extreme reactions. In between these rather extreme responses there are a multitude of arguments that ICT should be encouraging the reinvention rather than total replacement of schooling in the twenty-first century. Here, many academics, practitioners and even policy-makers are beginning to sketch out ideas for how ICTs could be used to update systems of schooling that have not fundamentally changed since Victorian times – therefore using ICTs to bring schools and schooling up to date with twenty-first-century life.

Most people would agree that schools have managed to retain many of the features they had when mass schooling first emerged at the end of the nineteenth century. Then – mirroring the factory and the industrial age workplace – it made sense to rely on an emphasis on physical presence, strict timetables and scheduling, and a general rigid organization of people and knowledge.[42] Now, however, the 'industrial era school' is seen to be unsuitable for the more advanced forms of learning demanded by the twenty-first-century 'knowledge society'. In particular, schools' continued reliance on structured hierarchies and formal systems of regulation is seen to leave them at odds with the challenges posed by new digital technologies. As Carmen Luke concludes, there is little reason in a high-tech age to persist with a model of schooling 'based on static print/book culture and competitive individualism where learning is geographically tied to a desk ... and old-style transmission and surveillance pedagogy'.[43]

All of these criticisms highlight what many people see as the pressing need to reconcile schooling with the challenges of digital technologies. Persuasive arguments have been made for developing teaching styles that are more aligned with the 'free spirit' of modern technology, allowing learning to be based around play, expression, reflection and exploration, and above all, creating rather than only consuming information and knowledge. It is also argued that if children are using ICT outside school to learn through collaboration, publication and inquiry, then these qualities could be better reflected in schools' systems of curriculum, pedagogy and assessment. Thus some educationalists and academics are now beginning to argue for various forms of 'e-assessment', 'mash-up curricula' and the refocusing of the teacher's role from provider of information to facilitator and guide.

Underpinning many of these suggestions is a belief that children should be given more control of their interactions with information and knowledge. For instance, Charles Leadbeater suggests a reorientation of the school to make learning 'a more peer-to-peer activity ... see[ing] children as part of the school's productive resources, not just as its consumers'.[44] Similarly, Marc Prensky argues for a 'new pedagogy of kids teaching themselves with the teacher's guidance'.[45] This sense of allowing young people opportunities to influence the direction of institutional change is reflected in Don Tapscott's blunt advice to 'give students the tools, and they will be the single most important source of guidance on how to make their schools relevant and effective places to learn'.[46] While none of these authors are suggesting the complete abolition of school, they are pointing towards a fundamental alteration and refocusing of what schools are and what they do.

Towards more realistic solutions to the problem of primary ICT?

All of these arguments contain some appealing ideas and certainly force us to think about how things could be changed. They certainly highlight some substantial problems and 'clashes' between ICTs and schools. Yet, all of these arguments can be criticized as putting too much emphasis on the interests of 'technology' and not enough emphasis on all of the other interests and influences that underpin schools and schooling. If we forget about the presumed priorities of ICT for one moment, then it could be argued that there are quite a few other compelling reasons to assume that the current model of formal schooling (however unsatisfactory) is set to continue for some time yet.

Although the current model of the school may not be perfect, its persistence would certainly suggest that schools are doing many things right. In fact, as Steven Kerr has argued, the continued persistence of the 'industrial age' school model could be seen as testament to the 'historical flexibility of schools as organisations, and of the strong social pressures that militate for preservation of the existing institutional structure'.[47] So it makes little sense – and is of little practical help – to argue that the only way that ICTs can be properly used in education is by radically altering the school. As Julian Sefton-Green has reasoned:

> Nothing is going to replace the importance of schools in educating the young in our society, nor is any other system likely to be able to play a role in overcoming social inequalities, but the formal education system is both under attack and in development from a number of directions and from a number of perspectives. There seem to be two main implications for schools and curriculum here. First, teachers and other educators just simply need to know a lot more about children's experiences and be confident to interpret and use the learning that goes on outside the classroom. Especially for teachers of young children, we need an educational culture that can draw on a wider model of learning than is allowed for at present. Secondly, we need to work within various curriculum locations to develop links with out-of-school learning experiences on offer. We have to find a way also of overcoming the fact that not all children have equal access to all experiences but acknowledge the real diversities in children's lives to support productive curriculum development.[48]

We would certainly agree with Sefton-Green's point of view rather than some of the more radical arguments described earlier. Whether one likes it or not, it makes little sense to reject the idea of the school as the principal site of children's education. Instead, it is more constructive to try to work with (rather than against) the notion of the school as it currently exists – for all of its flaws and frustrations. Instead of giving up on the primary school, it may be more productive to set about addressing the current technological shortcomings of primary schools in subtler and less disruptive ways. A more realistic approach to changing primary ICT could be seen as operating on a number of principles:

- working with what primary schools have, rather than what we may wish they had;
- working from where primary schools are, rather than where we may wish they were;

- working around the edges of primary schools rather than attempting to radically alter their central elements;
- looking for opportunities to adjust, tinker and loosen the structures of primary education, rather than completely rebuild and restructure;
- acknowledging what primary schools do well, rather than advocating complete technological change.

With all these thoughts in mind, it is our firm belief that if we are to develop some useful and realistic proposals for change then we need to pay close attention to the experiences, views, beliefs and ideals of those people who are at the 'sharp end' of experiencing primary ICT. In particular, this means talking with – and listening to – primary pupils themselves. Perhaps children may turn out to be a great untapped resource for primary schools when it comes to dealing with the pressures, priorities and promises of ICT.

Getting a pupil perspective – description of our research study

Overview: This chapter sets out the questions that we wanted to ask about primary ICT, and the ways that we went about getting answers. The chapter starts by outlining our key research aims of investigating the experience of pupils in using technology for (in)formal learning, and helping pupils imagine different ways in which technology could be used in schools. The chapter then goes on to discuss the advantages of using a 'learner voice' approach to answer these questions. An overview is then provided of the mixed-methods approach used in the research project to stimulate conversations with over 600 pupils about their uses of ICTs and their hopes, expectations and fears for future uses in the classroom.

Introduction

It is rare for adults to talk in great detail with children about ICT use. In particular, *educational* ICT use is certainly not a regular topic of conversation between children and adults – despite their mutual interest in making it better. As we discussed in Chapter 1, it is perhaps too easy for adults to assume that *all* children conform to the stereotype of the 'digital native' – using ICTs in seamless and sophisticated ways that older generations could not begin to understand, let alone hold an informed conversation about. Many adults therefore feel, quite reasonably, that there are many other important issues that they need to speak to children about, before talk gets around to the less familiar topics of 'pinging', 'tweeting' or 'questing'.

Put simply, talking with children about technology is not a natural thing for adults to do. Teachers, for example, will rarely have the time to listen to their pupils' experiences and opinions on ICT use. ICT will often seem to be a trivial and inconsequential topic in comparison to the other matters that teachers are required to discuss with pupils. Although teachers may well know a great deal about pupils' educational histories and family backgrounds, as well as their likes, pet hates and personality quirks, technology use will rarely feature in what they know about their pupils. Indeed, when we fed our research findings back to the teachers in our study schools, many were genuinely surprised by the responses from their pupils. In particular, many teachers were surprised by the depth and breath of what some of their pupils were using technology for, as opposed to the clear gaps in the know-how and skills of others.

Yet it is not just teachers who are unfamiliar with children's technology use. Parents also have little reason or opportunity to talk with their children about technology use in an open and attentive manner. At best, most parents will be concerned with ensuring that their children are using technology in safe and appropriate ways, meaning that conversations around technology will rarely take the form of open-ended discussions. Of course this silence is not solely the fault of parents. Many children understandably feel reluctant to talk openly with their parents about school and learning, let alone their technology-based learning. For many parents and teachers, education technology remains based on unspoken assumptions rather than informed discussion.

While teachers and parents have some very good reasons for not listening to children about ICT as much as they might, education researchers have far less excuse. After all, finding out about what goes on in schools is a large part of the job of an educational researcher. Yet perhaps more than all other groups of adults, education researchers can be accused of a double oversight when it comes to understanding primary pupils' use of ICT – rarely taking the time to investigate primary ICT at all, and even then *very* rarely taking the time to talk with primary pupils on the topic. Indeed, although there has been a lot of academic interest in education technology over the past thirty years, surprisingly little research work has been conducted on primary schools and ICT. Whilst there is a thriving literature on the complicated and compromised realities of ICT use in secondary schools and universities, the context of the primary school has received rather less attention from academic researchers. This tendency to overlook primary education stems, in part, from the assumption that teachers and pupils in primary schools enjoy a less constrained educational experience than those later on in the formal education cycle in terms of curriculum, assessment and pedagogy. Yet, as we have seen in Chapters 1 and 2 (and as most primary teachers will readily confirm), this assumption is simply not warranted.

Perhaps more surprising has been the reluctance of those academic researchers who *have* looked at primary ICT to focus on the perspective of pupils, as opposed to the perspectives of teachers, parents and school managers and leaders. It is likely that much of this tendency to overlook pupils comes down to personal interest rather than any deliberate decision. Most education researchers are former teachers or teacher trainers, and understandably are most interested in finding out about teachers' and schools' experiences of ICT. This is certainly reflected in the ever-growing academic literature on teachers and ICT, as well as the numerous well-attended research conferences and long-established academic journals that are dedicated to ICT and teacher training. For whatever reason, the fact remains that far less thought is given by education researchers to focusing their research efforts on the pupil experience of and perspective on technology use.

The need to develop a 'learner perspective' on ICT and primary education

It would therefore seem high time that researchers began to pay closer attention to the realities of ICT use in the primary school setting – not least from the perspective of the pupils themselves. As we have seen from our discussions so far, it is all too easy for adults to assume mistakenly that they 'know' what children do with digital technology. In actual fact, the realities of children's engagements with ICTs are highly complex and often contradictory affairs. As such, it would be sensible to argue that the ultimate success of primary ICT surely lies in schools having realistic and informed expectations of children and ICT. Perhaps most important is that these expectations are formed without relying either on overly romantic notions of children's expertise or on exaggerated fears of the unknown.[1]

In particular, it seems clear that primary ICT would benefit from better understandings of how in-school engagement with ICT relates to children's uses of digital technologies outside the classroom. In this sense, gaining an improved sense of the commonalities and differences between children's in-school and out-of-school uses of ICT should be seen as a central part of the effective development of schools' ICT in the (near) future. This point was emphasized by one of the major recent UK government studies of education technology conducted at the beginning of the 2000s – the ImpaCT2 study – that concluded that 'schools and homes have more to learn from each other about the ways in which ICT is being used in each context ... schools could usefully examine the ways in which ICT is being used in other contexts and whether these have any potential in the school environment'.[2]

Listening to – and learning from – the views, opinions and ideas of pupils themselves has become a rather fashionable topic in education over recent years. The development of learner-centred perspectives is now an integral element of the UK government's stated commitment to developing a more 'personalized' education system, with young people positioned as 'partners in learning' rather than passive recipients of education provision.[3] There is now increased emphasis on the notion of facilitating 'learner voice' – allowing learners to enter into dialogue and bring about change with regard to their schools and learning. Learner-centred perspectives have grown in prominence of late in educational circles through the increasing use of the 'learner voice' approach, 'participatory research' and democratic schooling. In all these respects, primary schools' use of ICT would appear to be an ideal area for such dialogue to be enabled and encouraged.

Although there is a tendency for such policy phrases to just add to our stock of 'buzzwords' and jargon, we would argue that there is much to be gained from taking a 'learner voice' approach to primary ICT. Of course, as Sara Bragg points out, there is always a danger that these activities become tokenistic or not truly participative.[4] With this in mind, we should remember that listening to what pupils have to say is only of value if you intend to do something with their suggestions. Some early advocates of the learner voice approach have observed that the recent policy emphasis on personalization and learning voice has led to students now being over-consulted in schools, but less often actually listened to. As Michael Fielding complains, many efforts to gather pupil voice in schools appear to be motivated by 'imperatives of accountability rather than enduring commitments to democratic agency'.[5]

Yet when used for the right reasons and with the right intentions, then the learner voice approach can provide revealing and insightful perspectives on primary schooling. For example, a learner voice approach provided a central element of the influential Cambridge Review of Primary Education discussed in Chapter 1. Here, research on pupils' views of their primary schooling was used to provide a realistic view of what it is to be a primary pupil at the end of the 2000s – often at odds with the carefree, unrestrained idea that many people have of primary schools. Pupils were found to often see the purposes of their schooling in mainly instrumental terms – harbouring concerns about the pressures of testing and large workloads. Pupils were found to be worried about friends, getting work 'wrong', the transition to secondary education, bullying and a general feeling that they lacked control over their learning.[6] All of these issues may be obvious to anyone familiar with primary pupils, but are not often highlighted in 'official' views of childhood and education and neither are they all equally represented in the media.

Given the success of this approach in exploring other aspects of primary education, we thought that using such a learner-centred approach could prove especially relevant to developing understandings of primary pupils and ICTs. In particular, it struck us that listening to pupils' views, experiences, opinions and understandings would offer an ideal counterbalance to the many adult fears that surround children and ICT. In this sense we concurred with a recent observation from the US social anthropologist Mimi Ito, writing about older children:

> Although youth are often considered early adopters and expert users of new technology, their views on the significance of new media practice are not always taken seriously. Adults who stand on the other side of a generation gap can see these new practices as mystifying and, at times, threatening to existing social norms and existing standards. Although we do not believe that youth have all the answers, we feel that it is crucial to listen carefully to them and learn from their experiences of growing up in a changing media ecology.[7]

So with these thoughts in mind we set about conducting a year-long research project that tried to address all of the issues, problems, potentials and pressures highlighted so far in this book through the perspective of the primary pupil. The guiding philosophies of this research project were simple. We wanted to spend the course of a school year developing rich understandings of how primary pupils experienced ICT in school and also at home. We also wanted to test many of our own assumptions about what makes ICT 'work' and 'not work' in school. As a result we were hoping to be inspired by pupils' ideas for altering and perhaps improving the primary ICT experience. In short, we wanted to design a research project that could allow primary pupils to have a greater say in the use of ICTs in their schools. As such, our research project was designed to do two things:

- investigate the experience of primary pupils in using technology for (in)formal learning;
- help pupils to imagine ways in which technology could be better used in schools in the future.

KEY ISSUE

Revealing our research questions
As with any academic research project, we had a set of quite specific research questions in mind before actually going into any schools. In this respect the project set out to address the following research questions in relation to primary pupils:

- What was the technological background of primary pupils in terms of their access to ICTs?
- How were pupils using computers and the internet in school and out-of-school settings?
- What ICT applications did pupils favour in schools and at home? Conversely, what aspects of ICT did they not like?
- How did pupils think ICTs influenced the way they learnt, both formally (i.e. learning related to school work) and informally (i.e. learning not related to school work)?
- What changes to ICT provision and practices within schools did pupils see as desirable?
- What types of ICTs did pupils imagine could be developed in the near future, and what forms of learning could they lead to?
- What qualities/capabilities of current ICTs would learners like to see continued, and what new qualities/capabilities would they like to see developed?
- How did pupils' ICT uses, perceptions and opinions differ by factors such as their gender, age, and school attended?

These research aims and questions frame Chapters 4–8 of this book and then lead us towards our recommendations in Chapter 9 for changes to the ways in which ICT can be approached in primary schools in the future. In the rest of the present chapter we now go on to describe in more detail the research processes we used to help us investigate these questions. In brief, our research took place in five different primary schools in England. In these schools we talked with over 600 pupils about their uses of ICTs and their hopes, expectations and fears for the future of ICT use in the classroom. We used a wide range of methods to get a rich picture of what pupils thought and felt about ICT – using surveys, interviews, drawing tasks and other methods which we will now go on to describe in more detail. Whilst further information along these lines may well be of great interest to academics and researchers, it is likely that many other readers may wish to skip the remainder of this chapter and move on to Chapter 4!

Description of the research project

In order to address the research aims and questions outlined above, we used what educational researchers term a 'mixed-methods' approach to data collection and analysis. One of the immediate decisions that we had to make was how much technology to use in our research activities. In following this mixed-methods research approach we considered it sensible to draw upon a blend of offline *and* online methods to stimulate conversations with young people about their uses of ICTs. While we wanted to talk with children in ways in which they were most comfortable, we did not want to rely too much on technology-based methods – especially if we were to hear from children who perhaps were not comfortable or experienced users of ICT. So for a research project with a 'high-tech' focus we ended up using a lot of rather 'low-tech' methods – although in retrospect some of these low-tech, paper-and-pencil methods worked rather better than their twenty-first-century equivalents!

Where we did the research

Having decided on *what* we wanted to research, our thoughts turned to *where* we were going to research it. We wanted our findings to be as generalizable as possible. Unlike many other studies of ICT use we did not want to focus on schools that we knew were making particularly exceptional uses of technology. With this in mind we tried to select schools that could be considered fairly typical of primary schools in England. We therefore chose to conduct our research in five primary schools in the London and West Midlands regions of England. We selected the specific schools to force some variation in terms of pupils' backgrounds – such as ethnicity, social class, and the type of areas in which they lived (e.g. inner city, suburban and small town). Of our five schools, two were inner-city schools and two suburban schools in London, and one was in a small town located in the West Midlands (see Table 3.1 for descriptions of each school).

Table 3.1 Description of schools included in the research project

School A: London inner city	This was a mixed-gender, non-denominational community primary school with 480 children on roll. The school was situated in a busy inner-city area amongst high-density council housing including some tower blocks in neighbouring streets. Around 2 per cent of children had statements of special educational need (SEN), with a further 23 per cent on the school's SEN register. At around 60 per cent, the number of children eligible for free school meals was well above the national average. The predominant ethnic group in the school was British-Bangladeshi, with Sylheti-Bengali the most common additional language spoken. The school achieved SAT scores above both national and local averages, with a value-added score of 94 per cent reported in 2005.
School B: London suburban	This was a mixed-gender, non-denominational community primary school with 430 children on roll. The school was situated in an area of mixed social housing but also close to an area of very expensive housing. Around 2 per cent of children had statements of SEN, with a further 15 per cent on the SEN register. Nearly a quarter of children were eligible for free school meals. Around 15 per cent of pupils spoke English as an additional language, with about the same number from different ethnic backgrounds with English as the main language. The school achieved well above local and national average SAT results, with a value-added score of 93 per cent reported in 2005.
School C: West Midlands small town	This was a mixed-gender, Church of England primary school with 220 children on roll. The school was situated on the edge of a small town in the West Midlands in a largely economically advantaged area. Around 6 per cent of children were on the school's SEN register, which is well below the national average. A very small minority of children were eligible for free school meals. Almost all the pupils were from white British back-

grounds. The school achieved SAT results above the local and national averages, with a value-added score of 100 per cent reported in 2005.

School D: London suburban	This was a mixed-gender, non-denominational community primary school with 470 children on roll. The school was situated in an area of mixed social housing. Less than 2 per cent of children had statements of SEN, and a further 27 per cent were on the school's SEN register. Pupils came from a very wide range of social and economic backgrounds and just over 25 per cent of pupils were entitled to free school meals. More than half were from a variety of minority ethnic backgrounds, with no one group predominant. Around 10 per cent spoke a first language other than English. The school achieved SAT scores above both national and local averages, with a value-added score of 96 per cent reported in 2005.
School E: London inner city	This was a mixed-gender, non-denominational community primary school with 240 children on roll. The school was situated in an inner-city area, with the majority of children from the high-rise council estate very close to the school. Around 60 per cent of pupils were entitled to free school meals. Around 2 per cent of pupils had statements of SEN, and a further 20 per cent were on the school register for SEN. Over 50 per cent of pupils were of British-Bangladeshi origin, around 30 per cent were of white UK ethnic backgrounds, and there were small numbers of children from other minority ethnic backgrounds. The school achieved SAT scores in line with national and local averages, with a value-added score of 100 per cent reported in 2005.

The four phases of our research process

Having chosen our five schools, we then had to decide how best to obtain data to address our research questions. The decision was made at the beginning of the research project to focus on primary pupils who were aged between 7 and 11 years and studying in Year groups 3–6 (what is referred to as 'Key Stage 2' in the education systems of England and Wales). In one sense this decision to concentrate on these older year groups was taken for us by the research funders, who were especially interested in the views of older primary pupils. Yet we also felt that the decision made good sense from a practical perspective. From our experience with earlier research projects it is often difficult for external researchers to engage kindergarten or early years pupils in conversations about their use of ICT in school. Although we previously had conducted research projects with some success with Year 2 pupils (i.e. aged 6–7 years), on the whole working with younger year groups had proved to be a highly frustrating process for the children and for ourselves. With this limitation in mind, we have taken the time to reach conclusions that we feel are applicable across the primary age span.

Having decided on the schools and the pupils, we then set about using four distinct phases of research activity. Briefly, these methods were as follows.

Pupil questionnaire

For the first phase of the research project we developed a four-page questionnaire to investigate pupils' encounters with ICT inside and outside the primary school setting. Questions were included to cover demographic information, details of ICT access and use, engagement with ICTs at home and in school, and perceived learning gains associated with ICTs. A final section of the questionnaire invited pupils to comment on how they thought school ICT provision could be improved in the near future. Questionnaires were handed out to all Key Stage 2 pupils in the five study schools by their teachers in class time during the autumn term of the 2007/8 academic year. As can be seen in Table 3.2, completed questionnaires were received from 612 respondents aged 7–11 from across the five schools. The mean age of the respondents was 9.1 years.

Table 3.2 Distribution of questionnaire sample.

	Per cent	_n_
School		
A: London inner city	20	123
B: London suburbs	17	105
C: West Midlands small town	19	113
D: London suburbs	28	169
E: London inner city	17	102
Gender		
Male	53	327
Female	47	285
Year group (age)		
3 (7–8)	14	83
4 (8–9)	18	109
5 (9–10)	31	190
6 (10–11)	38	230

_NB._ Summed totals may not add up to 100 per cent due to rounding.

Pupil drawings

The need to explore pupils' views, opinions and understandings in a variety of ways led us to also consider the use of drawings as potentially useful means of allowing children to express themselves. Whilst we were not sure how successful drawings would be, we were persuaded by the success of earlier studies with primary-age children which found drawing to be an ideal means of collecting data from children who perhaps found writing difficult or too time-consuming to get their ideas across. Of course, what drawings tell us is constrained by the skill of the artist and can only reflect values that are easily represented graphically. Nevertheless, the use of drawing as a method of data collection allows children a free choice of expression rather than being prompted by the researcher's frame of reference, offering those children lacking in literacy skills the chance to express themselves. With this in mind, a final section of our questionnaire invited pupils to respond to the theme of 'what do you wish that you could use ICTs for in school in the future?'. A 20cm by 10cm blank rectangle was provided for answers, with pupils invited to 'Write your ideas in the box (or draw a picture if you have the time or it is easier to explain that way!)'.

Once the questionnaires were returned we were very surprised by the pupils' positive responses to the drawing option. In fact, we received so many drawings that we have devoted an entire chapter of the book (Chapter 6) to analysing what the children drew and the many issues these drawings illustrate about schools and ICT. Of the 612 pupils who completed a questionnaire, 58 per cent ($n=$ 355) provided a drawing. As can be seen in Table 3.3, drawings were more likely to be offered by pupils who were in Years 3–5, and in schools A and B. On reflection, the success of using drawings as a means of data collection was one of the unexpected outcomes of the project for us, and one that we will be sure to continue to use in future projects.

Table 3.3 Distribution of drawings received from questionnaire sample.

	Completed questionnaire (*n*)	Produced drawing (*n*)	Produced drawing (per cent)
School			
A: London inner city	123	93	76
B: London suburban	105	71	68
C: West Midlands small town	113	48	43
D: London suburban	169	89	53
E: London inner city	102	54	53
Gender			
Male	327	198	61
Female	285	157	55
Year group			
3	83	50	60
4	109	69	63
5	190	133	70
6	230	103	45

Pupil-led and researcher-led 'focused-group discussions'

A third pupil-centred phase of the research process involved a series of group discussions using pupils and adults as researchers. As can be seen in Table 3.4, a total of 131 pupils took part in these discussions. During previous research projects we have always found focus groups to be a successful means of allowing children to express their opinions and views about ICT. In this project we were keen to allow children to talk amongst themselves about 'their' technologies, rather than feel constrained by having an adult researcher present throughout all of the conversation. With this in mind, we split the discussion sessions into two sections, and allowed children to take complete control of the first half of each session. We agreed with teachers that the sessions should be run during lesson time by pupil researchers (one boy and one girl in each year group). These pupil-researchers were pre-selected and trained during our initial visits to the schools. The pupil researchers each selected volunteer groups of five or six pupils in advance of each discussion session.

These group sessions lasted for 45 minutes (two 20-minute discussions, with a 5-minute break in between). The first half of the discussion was led by the pupil-researchers. They were given responsibility for conducting and audio-recording the discussion, which was run with no direct adult participation. Each group of pupils discussed three ideas for future ICT uses. In order to ensure successful discussion, guidelines for the session were based around the Key Stage 2 English curriculum guidelines for group discussion and interaction, speaking and listening – hopefully creating a discursive context which pupils were familiar with.

The second half of the discussion session was then led by an adult member of the research team and allowed the group of pupils to report back and reflect upon their discussions – thus initiating an element of reflection and dialogue between learners and adults. It also allowed for a number of more specifically focused questions to be asked of the pupils. This included questions on pupils' current and future uses of ICTs, their views on the transferability of their informal uses into more formal settings, and their perceptions of risk and suggestions for ensuring e-safety.

We found this method of collecting data with pupil-researchers to work well, with the children drawn particularly to using the digital voice recorders we provided them with – although there were occasions where some more forceful children took obvious pleasure in 'bossing' their groups. On the whole, though, the absence of adults during these conversations led to a range of issues being discussed that we may not have considered or covered. The scope of these discussions is illustrated in Chapters 5 and 7.

Table 3.4 Distribution of discussion group sample.

	Groups	n
School		
A: London inner city	9	48
B: London suburban	2	12
C: West Midlands small town	4	24
D: London suburban	4	24
E: London inner city	4	23
Year group		
3	4	24
4	6	30
5	5	29
6	8	48

Online/digital elicitation of pupils' views

As mentioned earlier, we were keen to explore how we could use ICT as a means of gathering data from pupils – especially some of the web 2.0 applications that support the creation and sharing of 'user-generated content'. With this aim in mind a fourth phase of the project used specially designed 'closed' websites for pupils to submit their ideas and thoughts about how their uses of technology could be better integrated into how schools use ICT. These websites were in operation throughout the fieldwork period and allowed young people to respond to the overall question 'How could we make the experience of ICT at school, more like what we are doing with ICT at home?' in three different ways:

- **Submission of open-ended texts**. One section of the website replicated an earlier study conducted by US researchers which utilized the online solicitation of student written stories detailing how they use ICTs at school and at home.[8] Following this research design, pupils were invited to submit a story of at least 100 words in length suggesting innovative ideas relating to how 'their' ICTs could be used in schools in the future. These stories could be submitted to a 'closed member' subscription space within the *Wikispace* website.
- **Submission of pictures/images**. A second section of the project website linked to a 'closed member' subscription space within the *Wikispace* website where pupils could upload drawings/computer-generated pictures illustrating their responses. In order to allow an element of dialogue, other pupils were able to view and to comment on these pictures.
- **Submission of videos/films**. A third section of the project website linked to *TeacherTube*, a free video sharing website for education users with high privacy settings. This provided a space where pupils could upload short self-produced video clips from mobile phones or digital cameras that illustrated their responses. Other pupils in the study were able to view and comment on these pictures.

We were careful to ensure that the websites were password-protected to ensure that access was restricted to pupils and teachers from the schools in our study. Whilst this method of elicitation would obviously attract a self-selecting sample of pupils who were relatively skilled, we thought that encouraging the production of user-generation content could help us enter into 'honest conversations' with young people about technology in ways that were meaningful to their contexts and modes of technology use. However, despite our good intentions you will not find any online data featured in this book – simply because these online methods elicited very little data from the pupils, unlike the offline phases of the data collection process.

Whereas it is tempting not to mention this apparent research 'failure', we decided to highlight it partly as a cautionary tale for other researchers contemplating using similar methods. We also mention it because, in retrospect, we think that it provides a neat initial indication of how ICTs were being used (and not used) in the primary schools in our study. Having talked to the teachers in the five study schools and having analysed the pupils' interviews and questionnaires, there are a number of possible reasons for the failure of our online research activities. Firstly, our questionnaire data showed that most pupils were not experienced in writing and publishing in web 2.0 environments. For example, although all schools in the study had static school websites functioning as notice boards and online prospectuses, it was not a part of the culture of any of the schools to compose online content in either blog or wiki form. At home pupils were most familiar with the process of looking at other people's content, rather than creating their own. On reflection we were perhaps asking pupils to do something that they did not otherwise do.

Secondly – and perhaps most seriously – the online submission processes we had set up were often compromised fatally by the internet security structures in place at the study schools. The websites were set up in the form of secure 'wiki' spaces designed for collaborative writing and uploading of pictures and video files. In order for the pupils' videos to be viewed within the secure spaces, they first had to be uploaded to a private teacher video sharing space. This two-stage process also required administrator rights to access the external sites. In most cases the wiki and the video sharing sites were inaccessible from within schools due to security protocols and internet filters.

In the light of these practical impediments, we offered schools an alternative method for collecting video data one month after the online sites became operational. We purchased digital video cameras for use by pupils in the project schools. These cameras were small, light and easily held and operated by children, even without any particular previous training in shooting video. The cameras could work in still or moving image mode using memory cards rather than tape in order to simplify further the storage and uploading of video data. Files could be moved easily from the cameras by dragging and dropping after connecting them to a computer with a standard lead. In providing the video cameras to the schools we encouraged pupils to make rough films of themselves talking about home use of ICTs, or else to film others using and talking about ICTs in school settings. Despite all these efforts, by the end of the research project only three of the five study schools had submitted any video content, and only two of these provided usable pieces. This suggests that a number of non-technical reasons also influenced the non-submission of data by pupils – not least the lack of time to create content for our project and perhaps an overestimation of the quality of video material required.

A brief note on our analysis of data

Before we move on to our 'results chapters' it is worthwhile to explain briefly how we made sense of all the data that arose from these different phases of research. In particular we should explain how we analysed the quantitative data arising from our questionnaire, and also how we conducted qualitative analyses of the data arising from the interviews and the drawing activities.

Given the opportunistic nature of our sample and the relatively simple questions of patterning which we wished to derive from the data, we decided that all the data were best analysed in a relatively straightforward manner. For Chapters 4 and 7 our analysis of the quantitative questionnaire data is described in terms of frequencies and cross-tabulations. Where appropriate, bivariate tests of statistical difference and association were conducted to gain a sense of statistical significance. However, in order to make these chapters as clear to read as possible, we have not reported these statistics in the text. Where the word 'significant' is used, it means statistically significant at a level of $p<0.05$.

As far as concerns the analysis of the qualitative data arising from the pupil interviews and drawing tasks, it was also our contention that these data were best analysed in a relatively straightforward manner. Following this lead, a 'constant comparison' technique was employed during our analysis of the interview data and drawings.[9] This initially involved reading all the texts to gain an overall sense of the data. All the data were then read again and open-coded to produce an initial code list until, in the opinion of the researchers, the analysis had reached theoretical saturation. From this basis the data were then selectively coded in terms of categories identified with the initial code list directly related to the research questions outlined above. Three researchers independently coded all the drawings, with a code attributed to a drawing only where all three coders agreed (which occurred in just under 95 per cent of drawings).

Conclusions

This chapter has taken the necessary – if sometimes dry and descriptive – step of outlining how and why we conducted our research in primary schools. Having established our research 'problem', and justified our strategy to address it, we can now go on to a more exciting part of the process – looking at our findings and considering what they mean in relation to primary ICT. The next chapter now goes on to look at our survey data. Just what were the pupils in our schools doing with ICT at home and in the classroom? How interested in technology were they? What were their likes and dislikes? How much of a 'digital disconnect' could be said to exist between inside and outside the classroom?

PowerPoint and penguins – primary pupils' use of ICTs at school and at home

4

Overview: This chapter presents the findings from our survey of pupils in our study schools. Drawing on the questionnaire data from 612 pupils, we provide a broad picture of how ICTs were being used (and not being used) across the five schools. We also begin to gain a sense of pupils' opinions of ICT use at school and at home. Although the survey found most pupils using ICTs, many children's actual engagement with ICTs was relatively basic and unspectacular. The most common uses of ICT involved games playing, chatting, retrieving information from the internet, using word-processors and making *PowerPoint* presentations. We consider why these findings contrast with the assumptions many people have for current generations of 'high-tech' pupils.

Introduction

Before we can make any judgements about how primary ICT can be improved in the future, we first need to know what is going on at present. To provide such an overview of ICT at home and at school, this chapter explores the findings from our survey of pupils in the study schools. The survey covered 612 pupils, and proved an ideal means of producing a broad picture of how ICTs were being used (and not being used) across the five schools. We also managed to gain insights into pupils' opinions of ICT use at school and at home. We will use other methods in Chapters 5–7 to examine some of the key reasons *why* these patterns exist. For the time being in this chapter we can use our survey data to address some basic – yet crucial – questions:

- **What kinds of ICTs do primary pupils actually have access to at home and at school?** Is it accurate to assume that all pupils are growing up in media-saturated households? If not, then which pupils are less privileged than others in terms of technology use outside the school?
- **What kinds of ICTs are primary pupils actually using at home?** Conversely, what kinds of ICT are they making little or no use of? Which children are more likely to have 'technology-rich' experiences outside the school?
- **How do primary pupils' uses of ICT when in school compare to their technology use outside school?** Are there noticeable differences and evidence of a 'digital disconnect' between school and home?
- **What are pupils' favourite uses of ICT in school and at home?** Conversely, what are their *least* favourite ICT activities?
- **How do pupils think ICTs influence the way they learn?** What areas of their learning do pupils feel benefit particularly from ICTs, and what areas are ICTs less likely to be seen to help?

Pupils' access to ICTs outside school

The survey first asked pupils to answer questions about what ICTs they had access to outside school. We were keen to see if pupils were living the 'technology-saturated' lifestyles that some commentators would have us believe, or whether children's exposure to ICTs was rather less extensive. In asking these questions, we were interested particularly in finding out about the ICTs that children could actually make use of – rather than ICTs that were not really part of their lives. In this sense we asked children to tell us about what ICTs they 'could use if I want to'. There is, for example, a significant difference between a computer that a child can use at any time, and having a parent's work laptop in the house that is usually out of bounds.

Thus, 89 per cent of pupils reported having access to a computer that was available to them to use if they required. Computer games consoles such as the *Nintendo Wii*, the *Sony PlayStation* and the *Microsoft Xbox* were also very popular, with 86 per cent of pupils reporting having access to one of these products. With so much written about children's 'bedroom cultures', we were also interested in the prevalence of television sets that were located in the children's own rooms. Overall, 61 per cent reported access to their own television in their bedroom – although this figure was significantly less for the youngest (Year 3) pupils. The other 'out-of-school' technology that we wanted to investigate was the mobile phone. Rather than ask confusing questions about who 'owned' or 'paid for' phones, we asked whether pupils had a mobile phone 'that you could use if you want to'. In this broad sense our data probably overestimate the prevalence of mobile phones in the lives of the pupils. Nevertheless, 51 per cent ($n=314$) of the pupils in our survey reported having access to a mobile phone that they could use if required.

These findings suggest that a large proportion of primary pupils do have access to these technologies in their lives. Yet it would be incorrect to conclude that *all* pupils have the same levels of access to these technologies, or that the children were all experiencing the *same* levels of technology use within their lives. In this respect our survey data pointed to some significant differences between different groups of pupils – in particular, some very clear differences in terms of age. As can be seen in Figure 4.1, levels of access to ICTs seemed to increase with age, with older children more likely to report access to televisions, mobile phones and computers. Only access to games consoles appeared to be fairly consistent between younger and older children.

We were also keen to find out whether there were differences in access to these technologies between boys and girls. Researchers throughout the 1980s and 1990s regularly highlighted computers

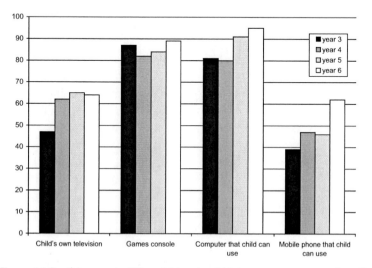

Figure 4.1 Pupils' access to ICTs outside school (data are percentages of pupils in each year group).

and the internet as being dominated by boys, although the more recent assumption is that gender is no longer a significant issue. Certainly in terms of our initial measures of access, gender differences were only apparent in terms of the games console. Here boys (94 per cent) were significantly more likely than girls (76 per cent) to report having access to a games console. Otherwise, no other significant differences in access to the other three ICTs were apparent between boys and girls.

We were careful to ask pupils questions about having access to ICTs such as a computer 'out of school' rather than limiting ourselves to questions about 'home'. We were interested to discover if pupils had access to computers inside their homes, or whether some had to rely on using computers in a setting other than their own home. In fact we found 7 per cent of pupils to be completely reliant on computer access in places that were not their own home. These 'other' places included friends' houses or the households of other family members (uncles, grandparents, older siblings). For some children, these computers were accessed through neighbourhood sites such as libraries, community centres, youth clubs and so on. In this sense, although nearly nine out of ten respondents reported having access to a computer that they could use outside school, only 82 per cent of the sample had access to a computer situated in their own home.

These differences may appear small, but the distinction is important. Nearly one-fifth of pupils did not have a 'home' computer, and we should remember that the freedom to use and the quality of what can be achieved on a 'shared' computer can be very different from what can be done on one's 'own' computer. These children would be restricted in many different ways – from issues of being able to save work to the hard drive, to issues of how much time can be spent online. It seems that a sizeable minority of pupils are 'second-class' computer users outside the classroom. Tellingly, these pupils who either did not have access to a computer at all, or had to rely on access outside their own home, were more likely to be in Years 3 and 4 (as opposed to Years 5 and 6), and were also more likely to be found in schools A and E (both located in inner-city London areas) rather than those in the schools located in suburban and small/medium town schools.

Pupils' access to ICTs inside school

We also asked pupils about what ICTs they felt that they could access inside school. We already knew what ICTs were 'officially' made available in the schools for pupils to use, but we were interested in pupils' *perceptions* of access – what they thought was available for them to use. Again, there is a large difference between something being made available to pupils in theory, and something being realistically available to use.

Our first finding reflected well on the study schools – with all the pupils in our survey reporting having access to a computer in school. The only differences between schools concerned the location of these computers either in ICT suites or in classrooms. Nearly three-fifths of pupils reported having a choice of using computers both in their classroom and in an ICT suite. For 40 per cent of the sample this access solely took the form of computers that were located in ICT suites. Only 1 per cent of the sample reported only feeling able to access a computer in their classroom, and not being able to use a computer in an ICT suite at all.

We also asked a question about where and when children had used computers in school – i.e. whether they could use a computer on their own or in groups, and also whether computer use took place only in lesson time or also in pupils' free time. The results were as follows:

- Have used a computer in a group in school during lessons – 67 per cent
- Have used a computer on their own in school during lessons – 50 per cent
- Have used a computer in school before or after school – 46 per cent
- Have used a computer in school during breaktimes/lunchtimes – 34 per cent

As well as showing the spread between computer use that took place inside and outside class time, these statistics also tell us how these types of engagement differed by pupils' year of study and the school attended. For instance, in terms of age differences, pupils in Year 6 (57 per cent) were more likely than pupils in Years 3 (47 per cent), 4 (44 per cent) or 5 (45 per cent) to report using a computer in school during lessons. Conversely, group use of computers was more likely to be reported by Year 3 pupils (81 per cent) than by those in Year 4 (64 per cent), Year 5 (68 per cent) or Year 6 (64 per cent). Notably, we found no obvious differences between girls and boys. Finally, as can be seen in Figure 4.2, all of

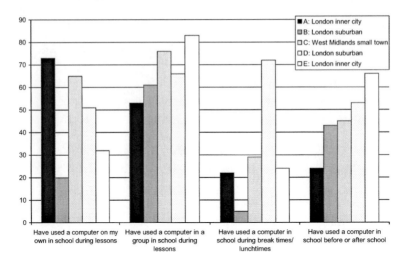

Figure 4.2 Pupils' use of computers in school (data are percentages of pupils in each school).

these modes of computer use varied significantly between the five schools in the study – especially in terms of out-of-class ICT use of computers.

Pupils' use of the internet

The survey then asked pupils to answer questions about their internet use, both at school and outside school. In this section we deliberately used open-ended questions to elicit these answers in order to guard against pupils claiming to use applications that they did not use. We were also keen not to miss out applications that we may have been unfamiliar with. There is always a danger that someone will tick a box on a questionnaire just because the option is provided (which is why some questionnaires contain 'fake' categories to catch people out). By asking pupils to list which internet applications they used we could be more certain that they were not just ticking a box for the sake of it.

In the event, our use of open-ended questions resulted in children providing us with a bewildering list of websites and online applications – many of which we were only vaguely aware of. As with television programmes and books, whilst many adults may be familiar with the online activities of teenagers and adolescents, a wide range of content is produced for younger audiences that can pass even the most experienced of adult internet users by. In order to illustrate the breadth of pupils' internet use (and also to help make sense of what the children talked and drew about in later chapters) here are some brief descriptions of the most frequently mentioned online activities that our pupils reported using.

- **Bebo**: a social networking site aimed primarily at teenage users, but catering for a slightly younger audience than *MySpace* or *Facebook*. As with most social networking sites, each Bebo user maintains a personal 'profile' where they can post information about themselves, their network of 'friends' and favourite music and videos. Other users can write messages in a 'comments' section. Options are available for users to decorate the appearance of their profile, and add a range of other material such as photo albums, polls and quizzes. Bebo is an increasingly popular means for bands and authors to promote their work through the Bebo Music and Bebo Books sections. Although most Bebo profiles can be viewed by anyone using the world-wide web, users under the age of 16 can only be seen by other Bebo users.
- **CBeebies**: the website hosted by the BBC for their television channel aimed at young children aged 6 years and under with a remit to offer a mix of education and entertainment programming. As well as providing information on the channel's programmes and presenters, the CBeebies website offers a range of activities for children, including games, colouring sheets, songs, stories and rhymes and a birthday section. A similar site is available for CBeebies' counterpart channel for 7–14-year-olds, CBBC.
- **Club Penguin**: a virtual world for 6–14-year-olds with over 12 million users. In Club Penguin children can navigate their own penguin characters (known as avatars and introducing a concept prevalent in virtual world applications for older users such as *Second Life*) around a snow-covered cartoon world. As well as waddling around, children's penguins can chat with each other, carry out tasks and play mini-games. At its simplest level Club Penguin is a free service, although to have access to the full range of features children must become paid members. Subscribers are able to use the Club Penguin currency to purchase virtual clothing, furniture and pets for their penguins.
- **Habbo**: a social networking website aimed at teenagers. Each child creates their own avatar whose appearance they can customize. Users can then visit a number of different virtual environments housed inside hotels. Some users will create their own hotel rooms as a social space for themselves and their friends that they can decorate by purchasing virtual furniture. Some children use Habbo to interact with friends and

other users in their own private guest rooms or in larger public rooms. Other users participate in online role-playing and play mini-games. Outside of the hotels, Habbo's website has a community section that provides regularly updated news and events relating to the site, recommendations for chat rooms, popular group pages and user pages.

- **Miniclip**: a website which allows users to play relatively simple mini-games, either as single players or with other online users. These games are usually produced by third-party software developers and change on a regular basis. The site hosts access to hundreds of different games divided into over thirty categories including 'Shoot 'em ups', 'Puzzles', 'Sports', 'Racing', 'Retro', 'Virtual Worlds', 'Dancing & Shows', 'Web Toys' and 'Five Minute (In a Hurry)' games. 'Brain Training', 'Learning' and 'Education' also feature as distinct categories of game, and a category of 'E-Rated (Everyone)' is provided for young children. Significantly, Miniclip is one of the few online services that regularly makes a profit, with an annual turnover of over £20million.

- **MSN**: the colloquial term used by most children for Microsoft's Windows Live Messenger – an instant messaging service that allows users to exchange short messages to each other if more than one of them is online at the same time. Messages will 'ping' up and conversations can take place.

- **Neopets**: a 'virtual pet' website catering mainly for children over the age of 6 years. Neopets is set in the virtual cartoon world of Neopia. Users can care for up to four pets – making their mood and health better through feeding them, reading to them and playing with them. The Neopoints virtual currency is used to buy food, clothing, and toys – with Neopoints being earned through different activities such as selling items, investing in the game's stock market or playing games. The site features a range of interactive and community features. Users can interact with each other through internal bulletin boards, chat rooms and email service. The site also features a range of ever-changing games, including titles such as 'Snot Splatter' and 'Barf Boat'. The site also features Neopedia, a *Wikipedia* type resource where users can send in articles, poems and stories about Neopia. Users are also encouraged to create their own stories, films and pictures which feature in contests and spotlight slots on the website.

- **Runescape**: one of most popular 'massively multiplayer online role-playing games' (MMORPG) on the internet, boasting nearly 9 million active users. The game is free to play and has relatively rudimentary 3D graphics, depicting the fantasy world of 'Gielinor'. Each player develops their own avatar and sets their own goals. Players travel through the different kingdoms of Gielinor completing quests, as well as fighting monsters and other players. Players can interact with each other through trading, chatting, or playing combative and co-operative mini-games.

- **Stardoll**: a 'dress-up' or 'Dollz' game designed for children aged 9 years and over. Each child is given their own personal page where they can dress up dolls in a range of clothes and accessories. Each user has access to an in-built chat page and can also access user-run fashion magazines and clubs. Stardoll also allows users to participate in virtual shopping where products can be bought from shops endorsed by real-life fashion designers and celebrities. Like websites such as Club Penguin, Stardoll is free to play at a basic level, although paid membership is required to access extra materials and tools. An elite group of 'Superstar' members are given access to exclusive material.

These nine sites and services were typical of the many online activities reported by the pupils in our survey. While these sites and services are popular with children across the world, it is probable that children in other English schools may have highlighted a slightly different list of sites. It is also probable that if we had conducted the research even twelve months after we did we would have been presented with a substantially different list. In a similar vein to children's taste in television programmes and pop stars, the latest online fashions, crazes and fads change amongst children at a rapid pace, making it almost impossible difficult to document.

That said, this list provides a useful illustration of the complex and overlapping nature of children's engagement with the internet. It was difficult for us to neatly divide these applications up into broader categories. For example, many of these applications featured the playing of 'mini-games' – short self-contained games that rely more on game play rather than complexity (they could be described as being more exciting versions of the PC 'desktop games' such as *Minesweeper, Solitaire* or *Hearts*). Many of the applications highlighted by pupils also contained chat and interaction features, as well as elements of social networking and self-presentation through personal profiles or avatars.

Rather than list each application separately, we have gathered them together by genre. Applications such as *Bebo, Habbo* and *Club Penguin* are categorized as 'virtual worlds/social networking sites'. We categorized *Miniclip, Neopets, Stardoll* and *Runescape* as 'games'. Along with Disney, Nickelodeon, CITV and MTV, we categorized CBeebies and CBBC as 'broadcasting companies'. When children

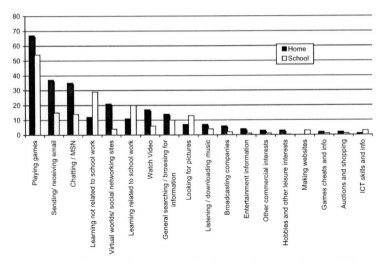

Figure 4.3 Pupils' use of internet applications at home and school (data are percentages of sample who report doing each activity 'a lot' rather than 'never' or 'a little').

mentioned visiting the websites of films such as *High School Musical* or bands such as Girls Aloud we categorized them as 'entertainment information'. We were careful to make a distinction (where we could) between 'learning related to school work' and 'learning not related to school work'. Despite our best efforts, we recognize that there will be some overlap between these categories. Much like adult users of new media culture, such is the converged nature of children's internet use!

As can be seen in Figure 4.3, we categorized pupils' internet activities into 18 main types of internet application. As we were interested in what online activities were important to children, we discounted anything that was mentioned as only being made 'a little' use of. Having made all these distinctions, our findings show that children mainly used the internet for games playing, chatting and communicating, finding out information (sometimes learning-related) and using virtual worlds and social networking sites such as *Club Penguin* and *Habbo*. Although highlighted in the interviews, only small minorities of pupils in the survey mentioned regular use of sites such as *eBay*, *YouTube* or game cheats.

As one may expect, the use of these different applications varied between school and home contexts. For instance, in-school internet use was more likely to involve school-related learning, formal learning and picture retrieval. Out-of-school use was more likely to involve game playing, email, chatting, watching videos, virtual worlds and social networking.

In terms of school-based engagement with these internet applications, use varied significantly by pupils' age and school attended. For instance, use of the internet for school-related learning was more prevalent with pupils in older year groups. Conversely, games playing and video watching decreased from Year 3 through to Year 6. Notably, no significant gender differences in school internet use were apparent.

In terms of pupils' engagement with these internet applications outside school, engagement varied significantly by pupils' gender, age and school attended. Boys were more likely than girls to report playing games and watching videos online outside school. Conversely, girls were more likely than boys to use *MSN* and other computer-mediated communication applications. Interestingly, use of games at home was found to decrease with age, whilst use of virtual worlds and social networking sites increased as pupils got older.

KEY ISSUE

The commercial side of children's internet use

Many of the internet applications mentioned by children in our survey raise questions over the increased privatization and commercialization of children's play and leisure time. Many of the most prominent and popular online services amongst primary-age children are commercially produced, for-profit services. Increasing numbers of most popular web applications are provided by 'media-giant producers' such as Viacom, which owns *Neopets*, and Disney, which owns *Club Penguin*. Many of the popular online applications targeted at what is referred to as the pre-teenage 'tween' market such as *Club Penguin*, *Runescape* and *Habbo* may be 'free to play' but all aim to make money from the users – what some critics term as 'pocket money pickings'.[1]

The commercial aspects of these applications are varied. Sites rely on a variety of tactics, such as tiered membership where subscribers are offered additional content, banner advertising and 'micro-transactions' where young users can 'spend' small amounts of virtual currency pre-paid by their parents or guardians. *Neopets* sells a range of branded merchandise through supermarkets, such as video games, stickers, notebooks, and a trading card game. As a representative of Nexon – publishers of the increasingly popular *Maplestory* virtual world – argued recently in the press, 'an in-game avatar represents an "ideal portrait of myself" in the cyberworld. Teens and tweens are very active in expressing their own individuality and do not hesitate to spend money on expressing it as well.'[2]

Pupils' use of computers for non-internet activities

It is often easy to assume that all ICT use now takes place on the internet, but our survey suggested that a great deal of pupils' ICT use remained 'offline'. As can be seen in Figure 4.4, nine main types of 'offline' computer application were reported by pupils, with levels of usage varying between school and home. Use of computer games, digital cameras and making pictures were all found to be more prevalent in the home than in the school context. Conversely, use of computers for writing, presentations, spreadsheets and databases was more likely to be school-based.

As with the internet applications listed earlier, we found pupils' in-school engagement with these computer applications to vary significantly by their age group and by gender. For instance, school-based use of computer games, programs on a CD, making pictures and email were more likely to be reported by boys than girls. Whilst the use of databases and spreadsheets increased from Years 3 through to Year 6, making pictures, using CD programs, digital cameras, scanners and playing computer games all declined in use as pupils grew older. Similarly, pupils' engagement with these computer applications outside school varied significantly by pupils' gender and age. Boys were more likely to report playing

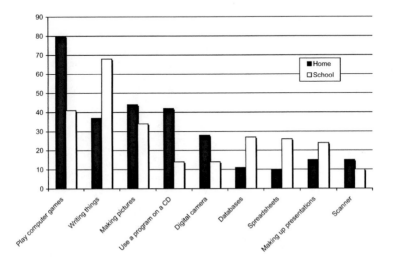

Figure 4.4 Pupils' use of computer applications by location (data are percentages of sample who report doing each activity 'a lot' rather than 'never' or 'a little').

games and using CD programs than girls while at home. Conversely, girls were more likely than boys to use computers for writing and making pictures. Use of games and CD programs at home declined with pupils' age.

Pupils' favourite and least favourite ICT applications

Besides finding out what pupils did with ICTs, we were keen to hear what aspects of ICT they particularly enjoyed (and what they did not enjoy). In this respect we used the questionnaire to ask pupils about their 'most favourite thing to use ICT for' and, conversely, their 'least favourite thing to use ICT for' at home and at school. Again, we used open-ended questions to avoid the prospect of pupils choosing answers just because they were listed. As can be seen in Table 4.1, pupils overwhelmingly cited their favourite out-of-school ICT applications to be games, with communication activities such as *MSN* and email proving a secondary favourite. Also mentioned, but less often, were virtual worlds, watching videos and listening to music. Games also featured as pupils' favourite thing to do with ICT at school, followed by making *PowerPoint* presentations, writing and art/pictures.

Pupils' least favourite ICT application may come as less of a surprise – especially for teachers and parents. Outside school, pupils cited their least favourite applications as homework, writing/word-processing, databases and spreadsheets (see Table 4.2). As far as school ICT use is concerned, respondents cited a similar range of least favourite applications – writing/word-processing, school work, databases and spreadsheets.

Table 4.1 What is your most favourite thing to use ICT for?

Rank	Location/application	Number of pupils citing	Per cent of pupils citing
	Home		
1	Games	237	39
2	Games consoles	40	7
3	MSN	21	4
3	Email	21	4
5	Club Penguin	17	3
6	YouTube/videos	15	2
7	MP3s/music	14	2

Rank	Location/application	Number of pupils citing	Per cent of pupils citing
8	Presentations	11	2
9	Writing stories	10	2
10=	Pokémon	7	1
10=	Chat	7	1
	School		
1	Games	159	26
2	Presentations/PowerPoint	37	6
3	Writing	32	5
4	Drawing/art	31	5
5	Internet	26	4
6	Maths games	15	2
7	Spreadsheets	13	2
8	Google	9	1
8	Publisher	9	1
10	Email	8	1

Table 4.2 What is your least favourite thing to use ICT for?

Rank	Location/ application	Number of pupils citing	Percentage of pupils citing
	Home		
1	Homework	93	15
2	Writing/word-processing	66	11
3	Databases	35	6
4	Spreadsheets	34	6
5	Games	23	4
6	Making pictures	22	4
7	Email	13	2
8	Subject-related games	9	1
9	Scanner	8	1
10=	CBBC/CBeebies	6	1
10=	Presentations/PowerPoint	6	1
	School		
1	Writing/word-processing	104	17
2	School-work	48	8
3	Databases	39	6
4	Spreadsheets	35	6
5	Games	18	3
6	Pictures/images	17	3
7	Maths games	13	2
8	Presentations/PowerPoint	12	2
9	Typing	12	2
10	Research on internet	8	1

Pupils' views on how ICT helped their learning

The final section of the questionnaire sought to investigate pupils' perceptions of learning gains associated with using ICTs both at school and at home. The self-report limitation of these findings notwithstanding, pupils were most likely to indicate that they felt they were learning from school *and* home ICT use in terms of finding out new things, learning to make and create things, and doing other things that they could not do before. Pupils were less likely to indicate that they felt they were learning from school or home ICT use when it came to maths, revising for tests or learning to read (see Figure 4.5).

Interestingly, although there were no notable differences in these answers between boys and girls, pupils' perceptions of learning gains associated with using ICTs both at school and at home did differ according to age and school attended. In particular, older pupils were more likely than their younger counterparts to feel that they were learning from ICT use outside school in terms of finding out new things, revising for tests or understanding ideas that they did not understand before. Perceived learning gains in reading, maths and understanding ideas were also found to differ significantly between schools.

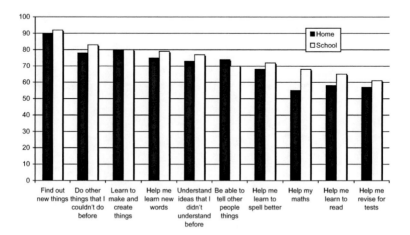

Figure 4.5 Pupils' perceived ICT-based learning benefits by location (data are percentages of pupils).

Conclusions

These survey findings certainly throw up a lot of interesting questions as well as highlighting some significant trends that we can further explore in our analysis of our discussions with pupils in Chapter 5. On one hand, our survey appears to depict a generation of primary pupils for whom ICTs are certainly an important part of everyday life. We found many children happy to use the internet at home for games and communication, while also able to use Microsoft Office applications for the production and presentation of their work at school. At first glance, these results depict a generation of children using ICTs both for play and for work – with their ICT use consisting of a blend of 'fun' applications such as *Club Penguin* and 'work' applications such as *PowerPoint*.

Yet when compared to the many claims that are made for ICT and education, it could be argued that these results show primary pupils' actual engagement with ICTs to be relatively perfunctory and unspectacular. In light of recent excitement over the changing nature of internet use, it was notable that creative and collaborative uses of web 2.0 applications were not especially prevalent either inside or outside school. If web 2.0 applications were being used by primary pupils then this usually involved the passive consumption rather than active production of content – for example, watching a video on *YouTube*, rather than making a video and then posting it on *YouTube* for others to see.

There was also a sense from our questionnaire findings of a distinct division between what ICT activities were taking place at home and what was taking place at school. School internet use was dominated by learning-related activities and picture retrieval. Home internet was dominated by online games, watching video clips and, to a lesser extent, chatting, visiting virtual worlds and usually social networking sites. Children's offline use of computers in school entailed mainly writing up work, making presentations and, for older children, spreadsheet and database work. In contrast, games playing seemed to dominate the offline use of computers outside school.

Indeed, the presence of computer games and gaming appears to dominate the ICT use of many children. Conversely, the least exciting and least favoured uses of ICT were for school-related 'work'. This distinction between 'play' and 'work' is explored further elsewhere in this book, and already appears to be an issue that merits serious consideration. With so much of pupils' (especially boys') ICT use taking the form of games playing, what room is there for more work-orientated applications? Does everything need to be disguised as a game, or do more sophisticated arrangements present themselves?

Aside from a general disdain for school-related activities, the majority of children did indicate when asked that they felt ICT use led to gains in learning – especially in terms of finding things out and what could be classed as self-directed learning. Interestingly, these perceived learning gains were felt to apply equally at school and outside school. At least two interpretations of this finding come to mind. This *could* reflect the benefits of school ICT use being 'cascaded' into the home (i.e. that learning benefits of ICT use in school were being transported over into the pupils' home use of ICT and replicated). *Conversely*, it could reflect the negligible role of the school in 'adding value' to how children are using ICTs. We should perhaps wait until we consider the rest of our data before reaching any definite conclusions.

Our survey findings are more conclusive in warning us against the assumption that all pupils are able to make use of ICTs in broadly similar ways. Even in terms of the broad questions covered in our survey we found signs of significant 'digital differences' within our group of pupils. In particular, the influence of pupils' age and school attended on their eventual ICT engagement was clear. For instance, pupils' ICT use was patterned clearly by their age and year group – from the quantity and the quality of ICT access to the frequency and breadth of eventual ICT use. Similarly, activities such as online learning, database and spreadsheet use increased as children grew older, with activities such as online gaming, chatting, making pictures and using digital cameras decreasing. Although older children were more likely to report perceived learning gains from ICT use at school *and* home, our data certainly showed the increased seriousness (and one could argue the increased dulling) of school ICT use as children progressed through Years 3–6.

It is also worth noting that consistent differences in pupils' ICT use were found between our study schools. The nature of ICT engagement in terms of what children were using ICTs for, when and where they were doing it, and with what outcomes, all differed significantly between the five schools in our sample. There are a number of school-related factors that could *possibly* be exerting an influence relating to the ICTs, including the physical location of the computers within the school; the curricular organization of the school; the experience of the teachers; the type of learning environments beyond the schools; and/or the range and depth of support from local authorities. One thing which was apparent throughout was the fact that ICT appeared not to be effecting a 'transformation' of the learning experience inside school in the ways which are sometimes claimed by education technologists and IT firms.

However it should be noted that our survey does not make it possible to pinpoint any causality relating to any of the factors above. In particular, it would be unwise to conclude at this point that any of these differences are somehow 'caused' by the schools. In fact, our survey variable of 'school attended' could be acting as a proxy indicator for a range of other issues, not least differences in socio-economic status, income, parental educational background and geography. So while we can note the strong differences in ICT use between children in different schools, for the time being we can conclude only that there are a number of issues this relates to. These are issues that become more apparent when we consider our discussions with pupils and their teachers.

It is now time to turn our attention away from the survey findings and towards some of the other research data we collected – especially the pupil interviews and drawings. This chapter has demonstrated how the questionnaire provided us with a useful 'broad-brush' picture of what pupils are doing – and are not doing – with ICTs. We now need to take a different perspective and develop more detailed descriptions of how pupils actually feel about ICT use, what their opinions and perspectives are on the importance of ICTs in their lives. With these issues in mind, Chapter 5 now goes on to discuss the data collected from the group discussions. Having ticked a lot of boxes on our questionnaires, what did the pupils in our study actually have to *say* about ICT?

Allowing primary pupils to speak for themselves about ICT

5

Overview: This chapter reviews our discussions with 131 pupils about their experiences of ICT use. Children described using a range of ICTs outside school – most often for playing games, chatting, watching videos and finding things out. Most children described these ICT activities as allowing them to have some choice and control over what they did, as well as helping them have 'fun' and be sociable. However, some children described ICT use outside school in less favourable terms – as sometimes being a boring, frustrating and disappointing pastime. Most children suggested that their school use of computers and the internet was more controlled and less inspiring than their use at home, although some recognized the potential for school ICT use to be engaging and educational. Above all, our discussions with pupils highlighted the clear differences between children's schools and homes as sites for ICT use. Yet rather than feeling disaffected and disengaged, we found that pupils offered largely pragmatic and realistic suggestions for changing their school ICT provision.

Introduction

In this chapter we examine what pupils talked about in our discussion sessions. We were particularly interested in what children said about the roles that ICTs play in their everyday lives. Letting the children talk amongst themselves allowed us to gain some rich insights into the issues that emerged from our survey data in Chapter 4. What were the attractions and outcomes for children of ICT use inside and outside school? Why were children making use of some aspects of ICT and avoiding others? What uses of ICTs could be seen as educational or leading to learning? What improvements to school ICT could be made in the future?

The children certainly found it easier to talk about their uses of ICTs outside school – especially in terms of describing the appeal of playing computer games. Many pupils talked in depth about what they did with ICTs in their free time, and described the pleasures and frustrations that they experienced when using ICTs. As we found in Chapter 4, pupils tended to be less enthusiastic and expressive about their uses of ICTs in school. There was certainly a sense that school ICT was not as engaging and 'fun' as it was at home, though very few children appeared surprised about this. In particular, pupils struggled to think of substantive ways that school ICTs could be improved. In fact some children actually objected to the prospect of more use of ICT in school. While many of the children's accounts were contradictory and sometimes inconsistent, a number of issues are identified which can inform our eventual recommendations for change in Chapter 9.

Pupils' use of ICTs outside school

As just mentioned, most of the children talked at length in the discussion sessions about their uses of ICTs outside school. They talked in depth about what they did with ICTs and the pleasures that were gained from ICT use. Interestingly, ICTs were often talked about in positive *and* negative terms. Much of what was said portrayed a sense of ICTs being used to distract children's attention and help them avoid 'being bored'. Children also described the downsides of their ICT use, especially the ways in which some ICT uses could be a cause of frustration or disappointment. In this sense the pupils in our study certainly did not portray their home ICT use in idealized or idyllic terms, and many were keen to point out that ICT did not dominate their free time. Talking with friends, playing games and sports, going shopping, reading and 'hanging out' at home with their family also featured prominently in children's day-to-day activities. Very few of the children in our study could be described as 'computer addicts' or 'games junkies'. ICT use may have been a focus, but certainly was not *the* focus, of their lives outside the classroom.

The choice of using ICTs at home

Most pupils talked with enthusiasm about the variety of hardware platforms and devices in their lives outside school. There was talk of using desktop computers and laptops (with or without internet connections), as well as games consoles such as the *Nintendo Wii, Sony PlayStation 3* and *Microsoft Xbox*. Some children were fortunate enough to own portable gaming devices such as the *Nintendo DS* and the *Sony PSP* (PlayStation Portable) as well as mobile phones and digital music players. Most children were knowledgeable about these devices. However, we know from our survey data that a significant proportion of children did not have personal access to them.

When it comes to what children did with these technologies, typical activities mentioned during the discussion sessions included:

- games (including those based on fictional characters such as Batman and Spiderman; sports and active games such as racing, fighting, football, shooting; simulation and role-playing games such as *Neopets, Nintendogs, Runescape, Cooking Mama*);
- watching videos (via websites such as *YouTube, Cartoon Network, CBBC*);
- finding things out (using *Google* or *Wikipedia*);
- communicating (using *MSN*, email, text messaging);
- writing stories and poetry;
- listening to music and stories (usually on MP3 players).

Children described engaging in many of these activities during their free time, often combining activities across different platforms at the same time. A child, for example, could be listening to music and playing a game on their computer whilst sporadically sending instant messages to their friends and checking their mobile phones for text messages. Many children talked about enjoying the flexibility and choice that ICTs gave them during their free time. ICTs were described as allowing children to be self-directed, independent and autonomous in what they did and when they did it.

It often seemed that this sense of flexibility, choice and control was a large part of the appeal of using ICTs. For example, in terms of games playing, online sites such as *Miniclip* were seen to give children a 'really good' range of 'free' games (boy, Year 5, School A). Handheld consoles such as the *Sony PSP* were seen to allow children to 'carry games anywhere' (boy, Year 6, School A). Online games allowed children to play games against the computer and with friends who were players of comparable levels of skill and speed. This was particularly appealing when the 'real-life' choice was to play with younger siblings who are deemed to have less skill and who 'you usually beat them on everything' (boy, Year 5, School C).

It did seem from our discussions that many children found it particularly important that they could exercise some choice in arranging their activities according to their own interests, desires, skills and competencies – as well as fitting in with their daily routines and locations. This is quite different from children's perceptions of their school experiences, and these differences will be considered in more detail later.

The 'fun' of using ICTs at home

When asked why they chose the particular forms of ICT use that they did, children tended to first offer broad reasons to do with ICTs being 'cool', 'good' and, above all, 'fun'. Although 'fun' can be seen as a rather vague and unhelpful word along the lines of 'nice', it does function, as Bob Jeffrey and Peter Woods observe, as a 'catch-all phrase used by pupils and teachers alike to indicate depth of involvement'.[1] In other words, pupils were indicating that ICTs drew them in and captured their attention – appealing to a variety of interests and motivations and allowing a degree of autonomy over what they did. For some children this depth of involvement was purely escapist. As one boy put it, 'you just do what you can't just do normally. And you can just go anywhere you want to go, there's such a choice' (Year 6, School D). This was especially seen to be the case when playing violent and aggressive computer games. As one girl reflected when talking about her favourite game, *Star Wars Battlefront 2*:

> Adult interviewer [Int]: I haven't heard of that game. Why do you like that one?
> Girl: Because you get to kill loads and loads of people.
> (Year 6, School D)

Besides the rather dubious appeal of shooting and killing, other children were attracted to what might be considered to be more homely pastimes. These included the simulation of cooking, dressing up and looking after animals. In particular, both boys and girls talked about enjoying games where they nurtured animals and pets:

Int: *What do you do on Neopets?*
Boy1: Play games.
Boy2: I feed my pet and make it grow and start playing games...
Int: *Is that what you do?*
Boy1: Yeah.
Boy2: ... and keep it living

(Year 4, School D)

Throughout their descriptions, children often gave a sense of engagement and immersion in ICT-based activities which some described as being 'in the zone' or in 'a bubble'. Whereas some children had performed these activities so often that they often 'didn't have to think' about exactly what they were doing, there was a sense of ICT use demanding substantial periods of concentration and attention as well as occasional bursts of excitement. Again, we can draw comparisons between these experiences and ICT use at school later on.

The social side of using ICTs at home

In addition to the appeal of having choice and control over doing things, some children also talked with enthusiasm about the social side of using ICTs. In particular, children talked of their passion for communicating, chatting and interacting with friends and other members of the family. Their eagerness for these social interactions certainly contrasted with the stereotypical notions of the 'anti-social' use of the internet and mobile phones that were highlighted in Chapter 2.

Older pupils and girls, for example, often talked keenly about using applications such as instant messaging and email to keep in touch and have fun with their friends. In the following example, two girls talk about the benefits of using *MSN* to chat and keep in touch:

Pupil Researcher [PR]: *And why?*
Girl1: Because you can chat to your friends, your cousins.
Girl2: Yeah I have friends all over the country and I can chat to them.

(Year 6, School A)

While our survey data highlighted the tendency for girls to favour activities such as chatting, emailing and texting more often than boys, our discussion sessions suggested that some boys were also eager to use ICTs for socializing. Older boys, for instance, talked of using ICTs to interact with their peers, family and occasionally people that they did not know in 'real life'. For some boys, games consoles and multiplayer online games playing were especially pleasurable means of socializing with friends:

> Int: Can you describe what you like doing about it?
>
> Boy: Because I play football quite a lot with my friends I just like playing [online] football games.
>
> (Year 6, School D)

> Boy: I like *Runescape* because some of my friends here play it and I like meeting up and at the weekends we can just talk and stuff on it. And then you meet other people from America and stuff and then you go to events on *Runescape* and then you play with them. I like *Stars Wars Battlefront* because there's lots of shooting.
>
> (Year 6, School D)

As these quotations imply, children could interact with other people whilst playing games online, as well as talking with each other about the games on other occasions – relating their experiences, swapping tips, tactics and means of 'cheating'. Although the interview data did suggest that girls were generally more enthusiastic communicators than boys, it appeared that some boys were also interacting through games rather than instant messaging and email.

The use of ICTs as a distraction

Apart from these pleasures of fun, flexibility and sociability it is important to note that children's ICT use at home was sometimes based on a 'push' rather than a 'pull' factor. Children also talked a good deal about playing computer games and using the internet as a means of avoiding the prospect of becoming bored. In this sense ICT use also functioned as a 'time-filler' and distraction:

> Girl: I sometimes use my iPod because I don't really have anything else to do and I sometimes use my iPod because I just like to listen to it sometimes.
>
> (Year 4, School D)

> Girl: When you're bored you can just go on it and just play games.
>
> (Year 5, School A)

Some ICTs were described as having sufficient variety to always alleviate boredom. As one girl enthused about the *Miniclip* online games website, 'there's lots of things to do on them like you hardly ever get bored' (Year 5, School C). However, other children described how ICTs could themselves contribute to a general sense of being bored. As these boys described, enthusiasm for a particular ICT activity could often diminish over a short period of time, leaving children feeling that they lacked more interesting alternatives:

> Boy1:   It's like if you're playing on it for like say an hour and you're thinking it's really exciting and then it gets a bit boring and then say that's the only game you've got and you can't do anything else because your mum and dad are watching TV and then you haven't got a TV in your bedroom or anything and your dad's on the computer.
>
> Boy2:   And your brother's on the laptop...
>
> Boy1:   ...yeah and you've got nothing else to do, it sort of gets a bit boring, you wouldn't know what else to do.
>
> (Year 3, School C)

Younger children – perhaps mirroring our survey finding that younger pupils made more use of games than older pupils – most often described this aimless use of games. Interestingly, some younger children would also talk about using ICTs to keep them quiet whilst adults 'were talking'. This suggested that computer games were being used in these children's households in a 'baby-sitting' role, similar to how television is often seen to be used in some households:

> PR: *That's fine, games console. Why do you like Nintendo DS?*
>
> Girl: Because it can keep you quiet when your mum and dad are talking to each other you can just play it and then you can keep quiet.
>
> (Year 3, School C)

The disappointments of using ICT at home

While ICTs clearly were a popular way for children to spend their time, the latter quotations convey a sense that ICTs could sometimes lose their attraction for children. Indeed, our discussions highlighted aspects of home ICT use that some children were less enamoured with. During the discussions, a range of 'downsides' to using ICTs was outlined. For many children, these issues related to safety and security – such as the fear that *MSN* accounts might be 'hacked into'. These are outlined in more detail in the discussion of children's understandings of e-safety and risk in Chapter 7.

Other disappointments and frustrations that were described during the discussion sessions tended to be rather mundane and procedural – highlighting the fact that ICT use does not always go smoothly or according to plan. Children related accounts of games not working as they should, batteries going flat, devices breaking easily, applications being too expensive and parents not allowing children to use ICTs as much as they would have liked. An interesting example of ICT being seen as something of a let-down was evident in the following excerpt:

> Boy: The thing bad about *Wii* is that some of the games they look really good but like *Monster Truck* game it looked really good but actually it was kind of – the colours, it was little cube of colours and it was kind of all fuzzy and it was really disappointing and it was quite expensive.
>
> (Year 5, School A)

This boy's response to the *Monster 4x4* game conveys a developing understanding that ICT products did not always do what they promised. It could be that this and other similar examples showed children having to develop what might be considered to be a healthy scepticism about the promises of ICT. It could be that these experiences might lead them to make more informed decisions about their consumption in future. In some ways, this capacity for developing a sense of 'digital discernment' could be seen as important as the technical skills required to use the applications or, perhaps, the beginnings of a more critical understanding of technology use.

Pupils' use of ICTs at school

When discussing their use of ICTs at school, pupils were most likely to talk about devices and applications that they were able to use on their own. In all five of our study schools, pupils seemed to feel the greatest affiliation with using computers for writing and drawing (e.g. using Microsoft *Word*, clipart and *Colour Magic*), information searching (particularly *Google* or *Firefox*), maths and science educational games and websites (such as the BBC Science website), databases and preparing presentations on Microsoft *PowerPoint*.

There were some variations between the five schools in terms of these preferences. In School E, for example, children talked about sometimes using the *Espresso* website (a dedicated educational resource). This school also allowed children to make some use of *YouTube*, unlike other schools where it was unavailable because of blocking software. Some children in School E recognized that this situation was unusual in comparison to other schools. They rationalized their school's access because they felt that their teachers needed to make use of *YouTube*:

> Boy: The reason why we don't block *YouTube* is because … they show kids like anything about racism or anything.
>
> (Year 4, School E)

Handheld devices had been used in School C for a technology project at the school. This school was also piloting a dedicated children's search engine that had been designed to allow children access to the internet. This search engine fulfilled a dual purpose of providing verified resources more rapidly than general internet searches, as well as filtering results in an attempt to prevent pupils accessing materials thought to be unsuitable for them. In other schools, children were keen to describe specific instances where it was clear that individual teachers had tried to tailor activities from the National Curriculum scheme of work around children's apparent interests. In the following example, Year 5 pupils in School B described their current use of databases to catalogue the details of toy animals:

> Girl: We're doing data handling at the moment.
> Boy1: Data handling.
> Boy2: Databases, yes.
> Boy1: Like we're sorting out data into different pieces so if it's like…
> if I'm talking about toys, if it's furry or not…
> Boy2: And different colours.
> Boy3: Different colours and what colours and…
> Boy1: The material.
> Boy2: The materials so we'd be sorting it out.
>
> (Year 5, School B)

In some instances, children talked with enthusiasm about specific subject-related ICT experiences. In School E, for example,

Year 4 pupils described searching for information on Henry VIII:

> Boy: You see facts on the computer and see if you can find more facts and print it out or anything.
>
> Girl: Or you could go to *Google* and go to images and you click on one of Henry VIII's pictures and there's a website that's underneath the picture and it says all about Henry VIII like when Henry VIII reached fifty his waist inch was 54 inches.
>
> (Year 4, School E)

Interestingly, it appears in this example that it is Henry VIII's seemingly excessive measurements (as least as reported on *WikiAnswers.com*) that have made this episode memorable. Similarly, games and play-based learning were remembered as occasionally converging in some school uses of ICT:

> *Int:* *Can you think of one that you can describe to me?*
>
> Boy1: Maths game.
>
> Boy2: Shooting Star times table.
>
> All: Yeah.
>
> *Int:* *What's that one?*
>
> Boy1: You have to shoot it to get it, it sends up 6 times 6 and the numbers ...you have to shoot it.
>
> Boy2: The correct number.
>
> *Int:* *You enjoy that?*
>
> All: Yeah.
>
> Boy2: BBC Schools and the BBC Science would be good.
>
> Boy1: When we click the internet it always comes up with the home page, BBC Schools and when we've got science it's fun, it's sort of like games but it's also learning stuff.
>
> (Year 6, School E)

Pupils also gave more ambivalent accounts of occasionally being allowed to use 'educational games' at school such as *Brain Trainer* and the *Big Brain Academy*. Generally these were considered to be 'boring' in comparison to their home games playing, although a few children admitted to playing *Brain Trainer* at home. The following excerpt demonstrated how children perceived these school games as different from their own preferred games. The main differences were in terms of having control and choice, as well as recognizing the 'educational' feel and purpose of the game:

Int: *How is using games different at school to using it at home?*

Girl: Because you're not allowed to use games, well only the
         games that the teacher lets you use.

Int: *How are those games different?*

Girl: Because they're learning games.

(Year 3, School C)

It was notable that despite their prevalence within the five schools in our study, most children did not mention interactive whiteboards to be an especially noteworthy part of their ICT use in school. When whiteboards were discussed, children described them as benefiting teachers rather than themselves. This was because many pupils felt that they were rarely 'allowed to use' whiteboards. Echoing their descriptions of ICT use at home, this suggested that some pupils perceived the advantages of digital technologies to be possible only when they themselves were in control of the technology:

Int: *What do you think about the interactive whiteboard, do you*
         think it's generally been a good thing?

Boy1:   Yeah.

Girl: It a good thing for learning.

Boy1:   It's a good thing for teachers because we don't get to use it.

Boy2:   I don't like it.

(Year 6, School B)

Acknowledging the differences between home and school ICT use

As should be apparent from these brief examples, in general pupils talked with much less enthusiasm about their ICT use at school than they did about their ICT use at home. As some of the quotations so far have implied, in many ways this is unsurprising given that ICT activities tended to be chosen more freely outside school on the basis of being fun rather than necessarily educational. Nevertheless, the perceived boundary between home and school – and corresponding gap between 'fun' and 'work' – was evident throughout many of the children's discussions about their use of technologies. As one of the children concluded succinctly:

Boy: At school you have to do work on the computers and at
         home you can play games.

(Year 6, School A)

In the same school, another group of Year 6 boys discussed how they would prefer more choice about how ICTs were used in their lessons:

> Boy1: I think there is a difference because in school sometimes we go to the ICT [suite] to do some work and publish work but when you're at home you can do whatever you like and you can play games as long as you like.
>
> Int: *There are times at school when you can do whatever you like though aren't there?*
>
> Boy1: Yeah but that's when you get free time.
>
> Int: *Would you like to have more choice in your school to use the computers, like if you could choose more?*
>
> Boy1: Yeah.
>
> Boy2: Yeah.
>
> (Year 6, School A)

Such responses are perhaps unsurprising given children's apparent preference for having choice and flexibility in their ICT use. The allusion to 'free time' when in school was also highlighted by pupils in School A who talked about the relative enjoyment of using computers for entertainment in 'Golden Time' that was described by one of the boys as follows:

> Boy: Golden time is when you're really good and you've done something that your teacher likes. Every day you have some free time and play with things.
>
> (Year 5, School A)

These discussions conveyed the sense that ICT use in school was sometimes being co-opted by teachers into wider systems of rewards and punishments – with pupils being permitted to use ICTs in autonomous ways only as a reward for good behaviour. This 'carrot-and-stick' approach to ICT use appeared to be marginal to the main teaching and learning activities of the school day and was certainly not seen by the pupils as being embedded within lessons.

Unsurprisingly pupils' perceptions of the limitations of school ICT use in comparison to home often centred on issues of regulation and control. In School A, one of the Year 4 girls talked about how she had limited access to *Google* at school – although she said that she used it a lot at home. Reportedly, her teachers had decided that *Google* should not be used in school:

Girl: Sometimes we go on there and maybe they black all of the
          pictures. So we only go on *Google* a little bit. We don't go
          much. The teachers had a conversation and stuff like that and
          they said you shouldn't use *Google*.

(Year 4, School A)

Whilst the teachers in School A would maybe contest the accuracy
of this perceived restriction, it is perhaps most important to
consider what children make of these restrictions and the implicit
messages they convey to children about the place of ICT in the
school.

Indeed, we were surprised to find a sense – especially amongst
older children – that many pupils appeared more sympathetic
towards such restrictions than might have been expected. Many of
the discussions suggested that children were aware of concerns
over safety and risk and understood that these 'adult' concerns
were a reasonable justification for limiting access to particular
applications at school. Indeed, children's ICT use at home was
likely to be limited by parents – albeit in different ways than school
filter and blocking systems. In the following quote, a Year 6 boy at
School D alluded to these differences by explaining that at home
he could do the same things as he can at school but that school
uses are 'safer':

Boy: I was trying to say, you can do the things you do at home at
         school but maybe different ones, the ones that hasn't got the
         same things at home, maybe the one that's got safer things
         on it.

(Year 6, School D)

It was noticeable that those children who had less access to ICTs
at home tended to describe school use of ICT most positively. For
example, many of those children without ready access to the
internet at home described the school as providing relatively good
opportunities for use. As this Year 4 girl, who was the youngest
member of her family, described:

Int: Is there anything you would like – any of you – that you do with
         your computer outside of school that you would like to do inside
         of school?

Girl: I want to do most instead when I get home, is like to have
         more time because at home I get less time because my
         brothers go on there for an hour and I go on there for half an

> hour. But at school I get more time so the best one is to go on the computer first before my brothers but at school it's better.
>
> *Int:* *So you get more time on the computer at school than at home?*
> Girl: Yeah.

(Year 4, School D)

Such praise notwithstanding, school was still seen by some of these children as a less 'free' place to use ICT than other out-of-school alternatives such as local libraries. The following discussion suggested that while using the computer at the library may provide better access than at school, there were still limits on what children were allowed to do. Even so, as the quotation from the second girl shown below made clear, there was a feeling that the library could provide more access than her school and help avoid the kinds of negative feelings that occurred when she ran out of time to complete work at school:

> Boy: Actually they don't let us do what we do at the library. They say we have to do what they tell us.
> Girl1: But all the time when we do work in school we never get to finish it and we never get to go on the internet and do whatever we want.
> Girl2: In the library we get to go on to the computer a lot but in school we have to get in time on it and we don't get to finish it, and if we don't finish it we get in trouble and when we get in trouble we feel really upset and then we feel like we wasn't appreciated and we done bad and we just let our teachers down.

(Year 6, School A)

Using ICTs for learning

As discussed earlier, the main benefits and outcomes of children's ICT use at home were seen to centre on issues of fun, engagement, sociability and avoiding boredom. Perhaps unsurprisingly, children were less likely to consider how they may have been learning through their ICT use. When learning was discussed, children's perceptions often focused on using ICT for completing homework rather than working in class time. Children talked about a range of ICT-based activities that they carried out for the completion of homework. These included searching for information and images on the internet, writing up stories and other project work on the computer, practising using databases and spreadsheets, finding websites that helped with learning times tables, and looking up words to find out meanings or spellings.

Finding out new information

Carrying out internet searches was mentioned frequently as both a home and school use of ICT. In particular, pupils mentioned using *Google, Ask Jeeves, Yahoo!* and *Wikipedia* to support their learning. Some children found it easier to search at school because they believed that computers were better set up for searching the internet:

Int:	*So is it easier to find things out at home or at school on the internet?*
Boy1:	School
Boy2:	School.
Girl:	And laptop.
Boy1:	School and laptop because it's all set up ready for you at school to find things.
Girl:	Yeah.

(Year 4, School A)

Conversely, others preferred searching at home because their time was less restricted:

Int:	*Are there any differences when you're researching stuff at home or you're researching it at school, are there any differences?*
Girl:	At home you can research what you want … but at school you usually have a set amount of time when you get told what you have to research.

(Year 4, School C)

In terms of what was learned from internet searching, pupils talked about how they developed subject knowledge as well as computer skills such as typing proficiency:

Int:	*What do you think you learn when you're doing that, if you're doing searches at school, what do think you learn?*
Girl1:	Learning to type quicker and learning different things.
Girl2:	It depends on what you're searching for. If you're searching for Henry VIII then you could do it and sometimes you could learn something.

(Year 4, School C)

Other pupils made similar connections, talking about how internet searching was a convenient means of developing functional information skills. Some of the children's discussions implied a degree of confusion around using search engines which related to how far pupils understood what they were searching for and how to best search for it. One of the Year 4 pupils in School E, for example, described an unproductive search session that he had carried out about sumo wrestlers. When inputting search terms, he had associated sumo wrestlers with China rather than Japan, therefore producing limited results. Other children's search skills appeared to be highly developed, as in the case of these pupils in Year 6 in School B:

Int: *If you had to find out about something like dolphins, how would you go about it in Google for example?*

Boy1: You would just type in dolphins.

Boy2: You would type in dolphins and if you want to find a picture you go on images.

Girl: Or web.

Int: *So you type in dolphins and you get a whole screen full of stuff and it's about the Miami Dolphins football in America.*

Boy1: You type in sea dolphins.

Girl: Or you type in like sea.

Int: *So you have to put other words in as well.*

Girl: Give more description about it.

(Year 6, School B)

Children's critical skills also varied in the extent to which they said that they trusted what they found on the web. Some pupils said that they tended to trust online information that had been found with search engines such as *Ask Jeeves* and *Google* as these were thought to be 'reliable'. Other children had more developed strategies that included cross-checking with other sites, asking parents, and only using websites produced by familiar organizations such as the BBC.

Enhancing written work

Besides using the internet for information retrieval, some children did discuss their creative uses of ICT – although this most often involved the use of ICTs to present rather than create work. A number of children talked about their use of computers for writing stories and poetry, creating Microsoft *PowerPoint* presentations, and typing up project work. Story writing appeared to be an activity that was often self-initiated. In contrast, project work and presentations were usually reported to have been work that had been set by the teacher. One girl said that she liked story writing in her spare time on her computer to 'use her imagination' (Year 6, School D). One boy described how he made up stories for his younger sister:

> Boy1: I just make up stories and write them down and I copy some from the book and let my little sister read them, I put some background detail into it.
>
> *Int:* *So you write some stories? Using Word?*
>
> Boy1: Using Word documents or sometimes I make PowerPoints.
>
> *Int:* *And sometimes you make PowerPoints.*
>
> Boy2: I like to play games for five minutes and then I go like do poems and do like Microsoft Word and Microsoft PowerPoint.
>
> *Int:* *That's very well organized. So you discipline yourself to just five minutes and the games.*
>
> Boy1: First of all, what I do…my little sister she first plays on it so then I have to wait for one hour then when she's done I play on the game site for only just fifteen minutes and then I go to Microsoft Word and I just make up some stories that I don't even know.
>
> (Year 4, School E)

Similarly, in School C, one girl said that she liked carrying out 'mini-projects':

> Girl: I like doing little mini-projects or things like PowerPoints or writing down things.
>
> *Int:* *What would you use PowerPoint for?*
>
> Girl: I once did one with a friend and we did it about animals and the RSPCA and those are the things that I do.
>
> (Year 4, School C)

Other children talked about how they used ICT to help them with ideas, check their spelling in Microsoft *Word* and to produce work of publishable quality. There was also a suggestion that pupils enjoyed being able to make formatting choices such as colour and font which they found satisfying:

> PR: *What is good about making PowerPoints?*
>
> Boy: It helps your spelling.

PR: *It helps your spelling by typing stuff, ok. And what about making*
        PowerPoints?

Girl: It's really fun

Boy: You get to choose what colour to print

(Year 6, School C)

Being able to present work neatly seemed to appeal, in particular, to older pupils and girls. Nevertheless, boys and girls appeared to be engaged equally in writing either for fun or for homework.

POINT TO CONSIDER

Telling tales with technology

We were struck by the number of pupils – especially girls – who used ICT at home to write stories and poems for their own interest and entertainment. Work on structuring stories and publishing them is a well-established part of primary ICT. Schools will use a range of applications such as CD-ROM story-planners and story-writers, *PowerPoint* templates and other software packages.

ICT can be an ideal means of helping all stages of the story writing process – not just the typing-up and publishing work stages. Consider how ICT could be used in the following activities:

- generating ideas for a story;
- working on vocabulary extension, writing style and narrative;
- composing and working on an overall structure for a story;
- sharing writing with others/collaborative writing;
- publishing work;
- finding an audience of readers.

Story writing could be an ideal area of ICT transfer where technology-based story writing practices and techniques can be introduced to pupils in the classroom, and then also pursued at home. However, this will only work if pupils can access and use the same tools at home as they have in the classroom, which is one of the aims behind the projected use of 'managed learning environments' in schools.

Instead of using specialist educational software packages that children are unlikely to have at home it could be helpful to take the time to search the web for free alternatives. It should be easy to find simple 'online story-generators' and 'comic book makers'. Microsoft's *PhotoStory*, for example, is a useful tool which is available at little or no cost. Some schools are beginning to use 'photo-sharing' applications such as *Flickr* for literacy development using handheld devices, provided that access is not restricted by school policies or local authority filters. It is also worthwhile to use applications in the classroom that children are likely to have on their home computers such as Microsoft *Word* and *PowerPoint*.

A less typical home use of the internet for languages was mentioned by Year 3 pupils in one of the London inner-city schools. These pupils spoke with great enthusiasm about using the internet in their free time for language learning related to the languages in addition to English that were spoken at home by older family members, including Bengali, Italian and Turkish. This self-directed learning, along with the spontaneous story writing described above, represents some of the activities identified in our survey as 'learning not related to school work':

> Girl: At home I play number games in Turkish but it goes a, b, c
>   but it's got a number so you have to get a, b, c, d in order.
>
> *Int:*   *What does that help you learn?*
>
> Girl: That helps me to do... a, b, c's for different letters, like
>   numbers.
>
> *Int:*   *So are you learning to speak Turkish?*
>
> Girl: Yeah. I'm Turkish so I speak some.
>
> (Year 3, School E)

Learning through play

Throughout most of our discussion sessions children, particularly boys, were very keen to try to highlight the educational benefits of their games playing. The justifications that were given often referred to the content of games, for instance learning factual information from games such as *Zoo Tycoon* and *Brain Trainer*, as well as improving their hand–eye co-ordination, mouse control and typing skills. Some boys argued that simulation games taught them to drive, fly, fight and defend themselves in the playground ('I can try out some of my moves', as a Year 3 boy in School A put it). Some children speculated that football games developed their team working skills. Boys and girls referred to games such as *SimCity* and *Nintendogs* as being useful for helping them to develop nurturing skills which included looking after people (*The Sims*); caring for dogs and other pets (*Nintendogs, Neopets*). In the following example, two boys reflected on the possible educational value of games such as *Zoo Tycoon*:

> Boy1:   Some games are educational! Say you have *Zoo Tycoon* or
>   something like that tells you about animals and what they eat
>   and things about zoos and it helps with your education with
>   animals.

Boy2:   You can learn about animals and what do they eat and what
do they do best in the jungle.

(Year 3, School D)

Other perceived learning benefits were perhaps even more
tenuous. One boy in School B reasoned that playing *Runescape*
online had improved his reading and spelling skills – although he
realized that not all the spelling he had encountered online was
standard. Some children speculated that games sites such as
Miniclip could perhaps teach a range of different skills:

Int: *Where a game isn't really designed to help you learn like on
MiniClip, do you still think there are things you can learn by
playing MiniClip?*

Boy1:   Yes.

Boy2:   Yeah – how to get your control of the mouse working.

Int: *How to score higher and stuff.*

Boy1:   Yeah.

Boy2:   And your typing it makes it faster.

[agreement from others]

(Year 5, School E)

POINT TO CONSIDER

Game on? The learning benefits of computer games in primary schools

One of the most frequently suggested improvements that children
and adults think could be made to primary ICT is the increased use of
computer games in classrooms. Since the 1970s many people have
argued for the educational benefits of using commercial 'off-the-shelf'
computer games as well as those games developed especially for
education. Many experts believe that computer games lead to a
range of benefits in the classroom – from enhancing children's
knowledge gains and development of psychomotor skills, to helping
teachers develop learning tasks that are motivating and relevant to
children's lives and cultures.

The problem remains that it is very difficult to identify any
attributable effect of games on children's learning – especially within
the day-to-day activities of the primary classroom. For instance, a
recent study in three Scottish primary schools used the *Nintendo DS
Brain Gym* game with Year 6 pupils over 10 weeks for 20 minutes a
day. The researchers reported noticeable increases in the game-
players' self-esteem, the accuracy of their mental arithmetic and
speed of calculation.[2]

However, it is possible that these increases were actually due to the novelty of using the games in classrooms that did not previously feature computer games. Even the researchers from the Scottish study admitted that their findings could be due to a general 'feel-good' factor and gratitude arising from the intervention. We should also be mindful of warnings from neuroscientists that adults using brain-training games to aid memory improvement may get the same results by simply doing a crossword or surfing the internet.[3]

Class task: ask your pupils to make a strong case for and a strong case against using computer games in the classroom.

Questions to debate:

- What do your pupils think about using computer games in lessons?
- What types of computer games do your pupils think could be best used in the classroom?
- When do they think would be the most appropriate time to play games and not interfere with other lessons?
- What learning outcomes do pupils think honestly that they would get from playing games?

Pupils' suggestions for change

It is clear from all of the discussions so far that primary pupils' understandings of their ICT uses tend to be rooted in their present experiences, and usually not focused on educational use of ICT. This tendency to see ICT in terms of the 'here and now' certainly limited pupils' ability to address our final area of interest – i.e. coming up with suggestions for the future improvement of ICT use in school.

At best, many pupils were able to only envisage ICTs being used in school as a substitute for their 'real work'. In this sense, some pupils were vocal in their opposition to the increased use of ICT in their schools. Rather than benefiting their education, these children saw additional ICT use as potentially distracting and detracting from their learning. The case against the increased use of ICTs in school time is illustrated in the following two discussions between pupils:

Int: *I just wanted to ask you, you were talking quite a lot about learning and some of you seemed to think that computers were good for learning and some of you thought…*

Boy: No they're very, very bad.

Int: Go on then tell me a bit more about that.

Boy: I think they're bad because you don't really focus on the learning side of real life, you just think 'oh let's go on the computer' and you do that for the rest of the day.

Int: Do you think there's anything educational about what you do on the computer?

Boy: No.

(Year 5, School B)

Boy1:   Like on the computer when you're sometimes playing games you could do mathematical games or science questions and stuff like that so you can learn more when you come to school you know a little bit more about the subject.

Int: So do you think that maybe there should be more games in school on the school computers?

Boy1:   Yeah.

Boy2:   I don't think so because it might interfere with real learning.

Int: So playing games is not real learning?

Boy1:   Well sometimes it is but other times it ain't.

Int: Other times it's just playing?

Boy1:   Yeah.

(Year 6, School A)

This apparent rejection of ICT use certainly counters the assumptions outlined in Chapters 1 and 2 about the appetite of the 'net generation' for technology-based learning. During many of the discussions children appeared sensitive to reasons why they should and should not be using ICTs in school. Sometimes this rejection of ICT use was based on simple matters of popularity. As this quotation demonstrates, ICT use in schools was not considered by some children as being particularly 'cool':

Int: What were you going to say something before about learning?

Girl1:   If you're on a computer and you get these programs like ICT maths and you can learn about anything you want to do with maths on it.

Girl2:   But the thing is hardly anybody wants to go on there.

Int: People don't like using it?

Girl1:   Except for geeks.

(Year 5, School B)

Other pupils also seemed to feel that they could not trust their own self-control, and would be distracted or act inappropriately if given access in school to applications such as instant messaging:

> Girl: Why *MSN* won't be useful is because if you're using it for work and you're meant to be telling a friend like 'can you help me on this', you're actually saying other things and you're actually being rude to other people, like talking about them.
>
> (Year 5, School A)

Of course, not all pupils rejected the increased use of ICTs in future forms of schooling. Other pupils were able to offer some concrete suggestions for changing their schools' ICT provision. Yet beyond the general feeling that ICTs could be used to make learning more 'fun', most children struggled to come up with practical proposals or ideas. In one discussion session, children considered the prospect of developing games that might help with literacy and numeracy skills, for instance, games that facilitated times tables 'fighting' with each other.

> PR: *So they can help you with learning at school with maths or – just maths, so how could you use it at school for learning, the game that you guys like?*
>
> Girl: There should be more number games.
>
> PR: *So what you're trying to say is that there must be more new games coming in?*
>
> Boy1: I think we need to get more games for learning and stuff like that.
>
> Girl: We need to do a game for maths.
>
> Boy1: We should just get CD-ROMs that teach us games about how to play stuff.
>
> Boy2: Show us fighting games but make them fighting times tables and breaking them down?
>
> (Year 4, School A)

Most of these suggestions for future change, however, involved requests for greater access to computers, using information retrieval more, having more time to type up coursework, having less restrictive filters and pupils being allowed to build their own websites. Occasionally more inspirational ideas were advanced such as when one Year 6 boy in School A suggested making podcasts of 'lectures' so that he could listen to them as he went to sleep.

PR: *How could we use it at school for learning? How could we use an iPod at school for learning?*

Boy: I think it would sometimes help to learn because I used to watch films, I forgot what was the name, but basically you know you have science like works and I did talk through lectures, you could get the lectures off the internet and put it into the iPod and then while you're asleep you could just put it into your ear and it goes into your head.

(Year 6, School A)

These examples aside, we were generally surprised by the lack of futuristic 'imagineering' amongst children. If anything, the pupils in our study displayed a far more realistic and grounded attitude to the prospect of technology change than many adults might have done. Although a few children were able to offer some suggestions worthy of science fiction – 'robots that can actually talk to you if you haven't got any brothers or sisters' (girl, Year 4, School C) – most were more realistic about the commercial nature of technological progress. As these pupils predicted, it was perhaps most sensible to assume that technology development in the future would promise 'more of the same':

Int: *What about in the future, you probably can't imagine this but sometime in the future you might have your own children. What sort of things do you think they will be using?*

Boy: It will probably stay similar but they'll make new games consoles. Stick with the name Nintendo probably because they've made a lot of Nintendo things. It will probably make it more like yourself actually being inside the game.

(Year 4, School C)

Girl1: Not really. I don't think it will be any different that much.

Int: *Don't you?*

Girl1: No not really. Only a bit upgraded.

Girl2: No more violent games?

Girl1: More than it is now but not much different.

Int: *So we're not imagining robots doing our school work?*

Boy: No I think it's going to be like in one thousand years or something that will happen.

Int: *So you think progress is going quite slowly then?*

Girl1: Yeah.

(Year 6, School D)

On the whole, then, pupils tended to imagine changes to school ICT in the future that were less concerned with the development of new technologies *per se*, than the development of new ways of organizing and managing technologies in school. As this pupil concluded, perhaps the most useful change to school ICT would be asking pupils what they felt that digital technologies could be used for in the classroom:

Girl: I'd get information off the kids and say how would you like the ICT room to be and then I'd get the school money into the things that they want and get more websites and the school website I'd put more things into it that kids will like want to know more about.

(Year 6, School C)

Conclusions

What is perhaps most illuminating about many of these discussions is how unspectacular and ordinary children's experiences of ICT were described as being. Our discussions showed that children's uses of ICT can be fun, but they can also be boring. Children enjoy being in control of what they do with ICTs at home, but often things can go wrong. Children resent the relative lack of choice at school, but sometimes appreciate being guided in their learning with ICT. Pupils are less concerned with spectacular reinventions of the school through technology than being given more of a say in how ICTs are currently used. Indeed, some pupils were not really convinced that ICTs should be allowed to play a greater part in their schooling. In short, most pupils came across as being sensible, pragmatic and considered users of ICT. This is not to say that they fully understood ICTs – especially in terms of having a critical understanding of issues of the authenticity, trust and usefulness of online resources and applications. Yet on the whole, the pupils in our study schools would seem to be far more ordinary and grounded users than descriptions of the 'digital native' would suggest.

Of course, it could well be that our findings from these discussion sessions were restricted by how we were asking pupils to think and express their thoughts and ideas about ICT. In looking back on the findings in this chapter we should acknowledge that it can be difficult for some children (and some adults) to verbalize their ideas and opinions in front of other people. With this in mind, we now move on to consider the children's drawings in Chapter 6. As we shall see, the drawings certainly provided some valuable additional insights into the issues covered in this chapter. In this sense, if we are to get a clear picture of the pupil perspective on school ICT use it is perhaps best to consider our findings from the survey, discussion sessions and drawing task together.

Drawing digital pictures: primary pupils' representations of the future of school ICT

6

Overview: This chapter considers the drawings produced by pupils depicting desired future forms of school ICT provision. We show how the nature and content of these future-orientated drawings reflects many of the tensions underlying children's present engagements with ICTs in school. In particular, the chapter discusses how the pupils' drawings offer valuable insights into the important issues underlying their understandings of ICT and schools. These issues include the restrictions of school rules and regulations, the differences between the 'work' of learning in school and the 'play' of using ICTs at home, and the unequal power relations that exist between pupils, schools and teachers.

Introduction

As the last two chapters have shown, primary pupils have a range of opinions on their use of ICT in school and at home. We have also seen that when given the chance, pupils have a number of ideas about how ICT use can be improved in school. Up until now we have relied on either directly talking to pupils or asking them to respond to pre-determined survey questions. As described in Chapter 3, we also used other methods of allowing children to express their opinions in an effort to ensure that all types of 'learner voice' were included in our study. Perhaps one of the most successful methods was asking children to draw pictures for us. Over half of the pupils in our study (58 per cent, n=355), provided a drawing in response to the theme of 'what do you wish that you could use ICTs for in school in the future?'. This chapter considers what these drawings can tell us about children's experiences of technology use in school, as well as their visions of future forms of primary ICT.

In this chapter, we use these drawings to address three specific questions:

- What types of ICTs did pupils imagine would be developed in the near future, and what forms of learning could they lead to?
- What characteristics of current ICTs would learners like to see continued, and what new characteristics would they like to see developed?
- What changes to ICT provision and practices within schools did pupils see as desirable?

When we analysed the drawings to identify the broad themes they covered, five main areas emerged, namely:

- the different types of hardware portrayed in the drawings;
- the different types of software portrayed in the drawings;
- the different people portrayed in the drawings as being involved with ICT use;
- the different types of activities which ICTs were being used for;
- whether or not the drawings displayed a futuristic portrayal of ICT use.

Different types of hardware

Pupils were most likely to depict what they wished they could use ICTs for in school by drawing hardware devices – most notably computer keyboards and screens, games consoles and controllers. It was interesting that although we asked for drawings of future technologies, the standard 'desktop computer' set-up of a keyboard, mouse and monitor featured in nearly half the children's drawings (see Figure 6.1 for an example). Nearly half the drawings also featured games machines or laptop computers. Older children were more likely to also depict collections of portable communications and entertainment technologies – with drawings of mobile telephones, digital cameras, MP3 players, and other personal digital devices featuring in these drawings (see Figures 6.2 and 6.3).

There were some differences in the nature of these drawings according to pupils' gender and year group. Games machines were especially prevalent in drawings produced by boys as opposed to girls. Conversely, girls were more likely to depict digital cameras than boys. As can be seen in some of these drawings, commercial brand names and trademarks (such as logos for *PS2*, *PSP*, *Sony SureShot* and so on) were apparent in a quarter of pictures of hardware artefacts, especially in the drawings produced by pupils in Year 5 and Year 6.

Figure 6.1 Desktop computer and mouse (girl, Year 3, School A).

Figure 6.2 Collections of portable digital devices (girl, Year 6, School B).

Figure 6.3 Collections of portable digital devices (girl, Year 6, School A).

A final category of what could be classed as 'other' technologies featured in 16 per cent of the drawings. These other technologies included a variety of existing ICTs such as whiteboards, PDAs, palmtop computers and so on. In seven cases children had attempted to draw more 'futuristic' technologies such as space-ships, tooth-mounted microchips, virtual reality helmets and so on (see Figures 6.4 and 6.5). Only in these instances were noticeably future-orientated forms of technology being imagined, otherwise children were drawing ICTs that already existed and that they were already able to possess.

Figure 6.4 'Computer helmet' (boy, Year 6, School B).

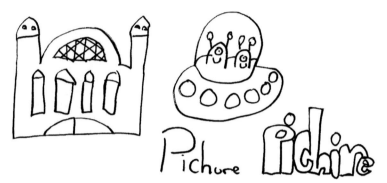

Figure 6.5 'Alien spaceship and mosque' (boy, Year 4, School A).

POINT TO CONSIDER

Using drawings to engage your pupils in dialogue

While often used by education psychologists and counsellors, drawings are a useful way for teachers to engage pupils in dialogue about improving ICT practice. You may want to ask pupils to design plans of classrooms or computer rooms that they think may make ICT-based learning easier. Another useful activity is getting pupils to draw 'mind-maps' which locate 'the internet' in the centre. Children can then depict all the activities they use the internet for in school on one side, and all the activities at home on the other side. These techniques can be useful ideal ways of understanding ICT use from the child's perspective, and make good starting points for further discussions.

Different types of software

Pupils were far less likely to depict their desired ICT use in the form of software applications (apparent in 16 per cent of drawings). This is perhaps unsurprising given the relative difficulty of representing software graphically. When drawings were produced, software most often took the form of vague portrayals of 'the internet' or else specific web applications such as *YouTube* and *Miniclip* (see Figures 6.6 and 6.7). Computer-mediated communication applications (e.g. *MSN*, email, chat) were featured in 11 drawings, search engines (notably *Google*) in 3 drawings, and social networking sites (*Facebook*, *Bebo*, *Habbo*) in 4 drawings. The commercial brand names of these applications were evident in 20 drawings (nearly all of which were drawn by children in Years 5 and 6).

Figure 6.6 'Mini clips plz!!! plz!!!' (boy, Year 5, School C).

Figure 6.7 'Let us go on YouTube' (boy, Year 4, School B).

People and ICT

A third theme emerging from the drawings were the people portrayed as being involved with ICT use. Significantly, just over a third of the drawings featured no people at all. This lack of people was noticeable especially in the drawings of the oldest children. Conversely, one in four pictures featured one child present, most often interacting with ICT such as sitting down in front of a computer or playing on a games console. Only 7 per cent of children drew more than one child in their pictures. Significantly, adults were included in only 11 of the 355 drawings, usually in the role of the teacher. This is shown in Figure 6.8, where a headscarf-clad teacher sits on a chair and is seen to give permission for a child to use an interactive whiteboard. Non-humans featured in four drawings. These non-humans included robots, space aliens, and other futuristic entities (see Figure 6.9).

Figure 6.8 'You can use the interactive smart board' (girl, Year 4, School A).

Figure 6.9 'Do my work now or else' (boy, Year 5, School D).

POINT TO CONSIDER

Why did teachers not feature in children's drawings of ICT use in the future?
The small number of drawings featuring teachers surprised us. Could it be that pupils wanted completely learner-centred and learner-driven forms of ICT use in the future? Could it be that pupils considered their teachers too old to be able to use games consoles and MP3 players? One way of finding out what your pupils think of you as a technology user is to adapt the 'Draw a Scientist' test. Ask your pupils to draw a picture of 'Mrs XXX using the internet', and then get them to explain and discuss their drawings. You may be surprised how your pupils see your technological expertise and style of teaching when using ICT. The discussions can be made even more revealing if you also draw a self-portrait and explain to the children how you see yourself as a technology user.

ICT-based activities

Alongside depictions of people and technologies, just over a quarter of the pupils' drawings featured discernible activities taking place via ICTs. These activities took three main forms. The most prevalent activity was that of play and other child-directed leisure activities – illustrated in Figure 6.10, where a picture of games-playing children is accompanied by the exhortation to 'do what you want'. Indeed, notions of play, free activity and other leisure pursuits featured in 49 of the drawings, most notably those drawn by boys. The portrayal of other activities was rarer. For instance, only 18 drawings portrayed communication uses, and no pictures featured noticeably creative or collaborative activities.

Figure 6.10 'Do what you want' (boy, Year 5, School A).

Figure 6.11 'Confused ... why don't you use the computer?' (boy, Year 5, School D).

Acts of learning and other educational activities were featured in 42 of the 355 drawings – most likely to be depicted by boys and those children in older year groups. Some of these pictures featured ICTs as supplementing formal education provision, as can be seen in the depiction in Figure 6.11 of computers 'help[ing] us learn if we don't really understand'. Less prevalent were more child-centred ideas of technology-based learning. While not completely clear, Figure 6.12 suggests a sense of free technology use which, as the child suggests, 'maybe ... could be educational?'. In this picture a games console seems to be flying through the air accompanied by exclamations of 'radical', 'education', 'cool' and 'bang'. To the right-hand side of the picture is a drawing of a figure with their hands in the air saying 'I'm the teacher'.

Another activity that was portrayed in two pictures was perhaps even more surprising – that of children choosing actively *not* to make use of ICT in school. As Figures 6.13 and 6.14 show, these pupils took the opportunity to depict their resistance to using ICTs in school, apparently based on the physical and cognitive strains of engaging with computers.

Figure 6.12 'Radical education ... cool ... bang ... I'm the teacher' (boy, Year 6, School A).

Figure 6.13 Technology rejection – 'You shouldn't use computers at school' (girl, Year 5, School D).

Figure 6.14 Technology rejection – 'I don't think it's a good idea' (boy, Year 4, School E).

POINT TO CONSIDER

Understanding the non-users of ICT in your classroom

Many technologists and teachers would be surprised by Figures 6.13 and 6.14. We did not expect children to respond in this way, but it is obvious from these drawings and our earlier survey findings that a minority of children are *not* very keen on using ICTs. There are a number of reasons why children may not like using ICTs in school. With young children the physical demands of typing, looking at screens and using a mouse can often be difficult. Yet we should not assume that reluctance to use ICTs is purely due to these physical factors. Some children may simply prefer reading from and writing on paper, and talking face-to-face. Others may be bored by computer use in school. The challenge for teachers is to be aware of different types of 'non-users' in their classrooms, and think of strategies to get these children involved in ICT, whilst remaining sensitive to the reasons behind their reluctance.

Visions of the 'future'

A final theme emerging from our analysis of the children's drawings was how the 'future' was portrayed. As all the drawings featured up until now suggest, the majority of pictures presented what could be said to be contemporary (rather than futuristic) portrayals of either home ICT use in the school setting or, less imaginatively, contemporary portrayals of slightly realigned school ICT use. Certainly the most prevalent view of 'the future' was the portrayal of home ICT devices and activities being brought into the school setting. This is illustrated in Figure 6.15, where a row of six classroom computers is joined by three popular games consoles at the side (a *PS2*, *Nintendo Wii* and *Xbox 360*).

Figure 6.15 Home ICT devices inserted into a school environment (girl, Year 5, School B).

It was notable that many of these suggestions for change adopted an almost pleading tone and were often qualified by a begrudging acceptance of school restrictions and regulations. This was evident, for example, in the labels that children attached to their pictures outlining a range of conditions to their visions for future change. Some of these conditions included:

- 'games at playtime instead of going outside at playtime' (boy, Year 5, School D);
- 'iPod then you give it to the teacher and she looks after it till spesail time' [*sic*] (girl, Year 6, School A);
- 'play games if the whole class has had a stressful day' (girl, Year 6, School E);
- 'ten minutes of time on the computer to do whatever we want as long as its safe' [*sic*] (girl, Year 5, School D – Figure 6.16);
- 'games sometimes (free time), MSN (if good) instead of reading, play on phone (if you are star of the week)' (girl, Year 6, School D – Figure 6.17).

Figure 6.16 Visions of change within the confines of the school environment (girl, Year 5, School D).

Figure 6.17 Visions of change within the confines of the school environment (girl, Year 6, School D).

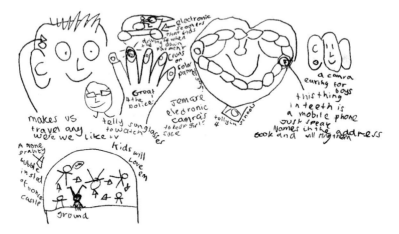

Figure 6.18 Futuristic artefacts in a child-centred environment (girl, Year 6, School B).

Only nine of the pupils' pictures depicted what could be said to be wishful, future-orientated portrayals of ICT use – six of which were drawn by girls. These pictures are exemplified by Figure 6.18, which features a variety of future-oriented products and practices. Here a number of miniaturized personal technologies are envisaged – from 'telly sunglasses to watch TV', nail-based gemstones which also contain 'electronic cameras to keep girls safe' and a corresponding 'camera earring for boys'. Perhaps most innovative of these technologies is the tooth-mounted voiced controlled mobile telephone and the zero gravity bubble-enclosed bouncy castle.

Making sense of pupils' drawings

We hope that the examples in this chapter demonstrate the value of using drawings to enable pupils' expression of their under-standings, opinions and experiences of ICT – supporting Diane Mavers' assertion that 'the potentialities of drawing may enable new things to be communicated, or the "same" things to be expressed in a different way'.[1] Indeed, many of the children in our study were able to produce drawings about ICTs and schools that were emotionally expressive, as well as conveying quite complex notions about ICTs and the school setting. Of course these responses must be seen in light of the context in which the drawing occurred. It could well be that the production of drawings through an 'artificial' research task conducted in school will have shaped pupil responses. Yet within the limitations of the data collection process, we would contend that the drawings featured in this chapter offer some valuable insights into ICTs, schools and the experiences of primary pupils.

For instance, with reference to the questions posed at the beginning of the chapter, it was notable that children's perceptions of future forms of education were remarkably mundane, rooted in the present-day context of the classroom and constrained by school rules, regulations and expectations. In contrast to some educationalists' excitement over the use of futuristic technologies such as robots in the classroom, our pupils' visions for change in school ICT provision were mostly concerned with the direct importing of 'home' ICT devices and play activities in the classroom.[2] Significantly, there was little sense of a strong desire for change regarding pupils' learning with ICTs.

Similarly, in terms of what types of ICTs pupils imagined would be developed in the near future and what forms of learning they could lead to, few new developments were offered aside from the occasional drawing of a zero-gravity bouncy castle or virtual reality helmet. Given the persistent presence of the PC in schools'

ICT provision, imagining the near future in terms of the standard desktop computer set-up of keyboard, mouse and monitor is perhaps a sensible assumption. In the drawings where children were depicting technology-based learning, ICTs were portrayed as being used to help children when confused, relieve children from the stresses of learning in the classroom or else lead to incidental learning (although these latter suggestions were often offered as a tentative justification; as the child who drew the 'radical education' drawing (Figure 6.10) wondered, 'maybe it could be educational?').

As to the desired characteristics of ICT use in the future, children's drawings were concerned primarily with issues of play, fun, portability and the personal ownership of hardware devices. These qualities and capabilities were seen to be best achieved by 'importing' children's own home technologies into the school, most notably games consoles, and, for older children, mobile phones, digital cameras and MP3 players. Finally, in terms of desired changes to ICT provision and practices within schools, the majority of drawings which advocated change depicted the removal (or at least relaxation) of restrictions of use imposed by the school – as a few pictures put it, 'let us do what we want'. Significantly, letting pupils 'do what they want' most often involved the playing of games or passive 'going on' websites such as *YouTube* or *Miniclip*. There were few, if any, portrayals of the more communicative, creative or collaborative ICT practices associated with web 2.0 applications.

Despite the slightly unimaginative nature of some of the responses, it would be unwise to dismiss these drawings as uninformed or somehow missing the point of the exercise. Instead we would contend that these drawings of a desired future reflect many of the tensions that were also highlighted in our discussions with children regarding their current ICT use in school. In particular, many of these drawings reflect clearly the restrictions of the school as opposed to the (relative) freedoms of the home. Often this was portrayed in terms of the oppositional relationship between the 'work' of learning in school and the 'play' of using digital technologies at home.

Another theme running throughout many of these drawings is the unequal power relations that exist between pupils, schools, teachers, and their homes. In all these instances, the drawings provide stark depictions of how ICTs are restricted by primary schools, not least the day-to-day concerns that schools have such as delivering national curriculum content, timetabling, filtering content and so on. In this sense, these drawings demonstrate how children's aspirations for school ICT provision are influenced by the organizational contexts of schools in which they are located.

It could be argued that digital devices such as games consoles, mobile telephones and MP3 players act as modest totems of individualized resistance for children – although most children seemed well aware that such devices could not transgress easily into the school environment. From this perspective it is understandable that the main advantage of ICTs for these primary pupils was not seen to be associated with learning, but rather the ability to imagine some form of increased freedom within the confines of formal education. Whilst perhaps unsurprising, this conclusion does have some serious implications for teachers and schools who want to consult with young people with regard to future forms of ICT provision that are of educational and pedagogic value.

This may well explain why the majority of pupils in our study were either reluctant or unable to imagine any alternative forms of educational ICT provision other than the unrestricted importing of home ICT artefacts and activities into the school. It could be that these drawings also reflect the fact that 'ICT-savvy' children are also profoundly 'school-savvy' children. We have seen from the drawings in this chapter how many children understand that ICTs are regulated within school, as are most aspects of their lives. As such, the limited forms of ICT use reported in our study are just one instance of the many restrictions that are imposed on children whilst in school – from the restrictions of school uniforms and school meals, to the restrictions of the school timetable. We would contend that the reluctance to imagine radically different visions of 'the future' reflected in our pupils' drawings is perhaps rooted in the regulated nature of the primary school environment and the pervasive effect that school structures have on pupils' experiences.

POINT TO CONSIDER

Why there were so few 'futuristic' drawings in our study?
One of the most surprising features of this part of our study was the lack of distinctly futuristic drawings. As explained below, we suspect that this reflects children's realistic understanding of how difficult it is to effect change in schools, certainly from their perspective. However, there could be alternative explanations. It could be that this reluctance to imagine future forms of educational ICT provision simply confirms the 'familiarity hypothesis' that most children will always reflect their direct experiences in any drawings. Alternatively, it could simply be that most children in Key Stage 2 are unable to conceptualize future change and are absorbed in their varied and demanding day-to-day experiences of lived culture. Conversely, the lack of future-orientated 'imagineering' in our pupils' drawings could indicate a general indifference to thinking about school, or even taking part in the research project!

Conclusions

Of course this somewhat bleak conclusion offers little encouragement for those seeking to involve learners in the design and development of future forms of ICT. Clearly, the drawings in our study offer few suggestions for the development of meaningful and educationally acceptable future forms of educational ICT. What the drawings illustrate most comprehensively are the differences between school and home that children and ICTs are currently caught within. In this sense the drawings are an appropriate preparation for our conclusions and recommendations in Chapter 9. It would seem from these children's drawings that there is no magical and instant 'technological fix' that teachers and schools have somehow overlooked until now. Apart from the predictable demands to 'let us do what we want', pupils expressed few clear demands for specific changes in their drawings. It would seem that any solution to the 'ICT problem' in primary schools is perhaps far more fundamental than designing new forms of technology.

Primary pupils' experiences and understandings of 'e-safety'

Overview: This chapter looks again at our survey and discussions with pupils to examine pupils' experiences and understandings of managing issues of risk and safety during their use of ICTs. We find that while most children recognize the need to be mindful of ICT-related risks and dangers, their personal experiences of actual risks tend to be framed in terms of operational problems encountered when using ICTs. Conversely, pupils' understandings of potential risk were often based upon exaggerated fears deriving from urban myths and moral panics relating to child safety. These findings suggest that official notions of 'e-safety' remain abstract and poorly understood concepts for many of the children in our study.

Introduction

As outlined in Chapter 1, many people see ICTs as a potential benefit but also as a potential threat to children. Although many advantages are felt to arise from children's use of ICT, parents, teachers and policy-makers remain concerned that these benefits are compromised by a number of *risks* associated with ICT use. These risks and dangers are many – from the range of adult content that can be accessed easily online, to the potential for making inappropriate contact with others. Adult fears often centre on the risk of children being exposed inadvertently to undesirable violent or sexual content, as well as predatory adults. Stories abound in the media about online grooming of children by paedophiles. There is also a risk of children 'knowingly' using ICTs to put either themselves or others at risk – often by actively engaging in illicit experiences away from the regulation of adults.

Many people's concerns are heightened by the fact that there is apparently very little that adults can do to intervene. Politicians and other organizations will sporadically float ideas such as the idea of cinema-style age ratings for websites and fund task forces on online children protection, but such interventions are often suggested more in hope than certainty that such initiatives will work. Despite its obvious benefits, ICT is often seen as one of the more unpleasant aspects of growing up in the twenty-first century. In this sense technologies such as the internet and mobile phone have been positioned at the centre of the so-called 'toxic childhood' argument where the social, emotional and cognitive development of a growing number of children is seen to have been damaged by the increasing presence of the adult world and adult interests in the lives of children.[1]

While perhaps overly alarmist and reactionary, there are some grounds for taking these arguments seriously. If we consider the growing presence of commercial concerns in children's lives, for example, then ICT would appear to be a key arena where risks as well as benefits for childhood exist. Recent concerns have been raised over the exploitation of children's interest in ICT by advertisers and marketeers – with much of what young people engage with on the internet carrying a latent (and sometimes blatant) agenda of brand awareness, product placement and viral advertising. It has been estimated that up to 85 per cent of websites used by the lucrative 'tween' market of 5–12-year-olds collect data on users' postcodes, dates of birth and email addresses. Over one-third of children's websites are estimated to offer incentives for users to provide further personal information.[2] Such 'grooming' of young consumers is typified by the 17 million users of *Stardoll*, who are encouraged to dress and accessorize their doll avatars from virtual designer outlets stocked with the likes of DKNY and Jordache.

All of these examples highlight the extent of the risks and dangers associated with children's use of ICT. As such, the last decade has seen growing concern amongst policy-makers and practitioners over ICTs as 'a new medium for the victimization of children',[3] with many people recognizing the need to encourage children's 'safe' use of ICTs in school, home and community settings. As we discussed briefly in Chapter 1, 'e-safety' has become one of the 'big' pressures and priorities for primary schools and teachers.

Definitions of ICT-related risks and dangers

There has been much discussion in the UK school sector on the topic of 'e-safety'. Official definitions of 'e-safety' start from the following assumption:

> children and young people are vulnerable and may expose themselves to danger – knowingly or unknowingly – when using the internet and other digital technologies. Indeed, some young people may find themselves involved in activities that are inappropriate or possibly illegal.[4]

In particular, official guidance from the UK government to schools highlights a number of specific 'e-safety' risks and dangers centred on 'four Cs' of online content, contact, commerce and culture. From this perspective children are felt to require protection from risks such as cyber-bullying, exposure to online paedophiles, violent games, illicit downloading of material and the dangers associated with disclosure of personal information. In these terms, ensuring the safety of pupils' school use of ICTs – and the internet in particular – is now a key concern for educators.

KEY ISSUE

UK government categorization of 'e-safety risks'

Content
- Exposure to age-inappropriate material
- Exposure to inaccurate or misleading information
- Exposure to socially unacceptable material, such as that inciting violence, hate or intolerance
- Exposure to illegal material, such as images of child abuse

Contact
- Grooming using communication technologies, leading to sexual assault and/or child prostitution

Commerce
- Exposure of minors to inappropriate commercial advertising
- Exposure to online gambling services
- Commercial and financial scams

Culture
- Bullying via websites, mobile phones or other forms of communication device
- Downloading of copyrighted materials, e.g. music and films

This official definition of 'e-safety' has been supported by a succession of government policies and initiatives – starting in the late 1990s with the introduction of the Superhighway Safety and GridWatch initiatives. Now under official guidelines schools are expected to develop 'safe e-learning environments' through developing their own internet codes of 'acceptable use', providing guidance on e-safety for pupils and staff and, where possible, assigning teachers as dedicated 'internet safety co-ordinators' and using appropriate monitoring and filtering software. In particular, school governors are expected to oversee the development and implementation of school e-safety policies.

These school-focused interventions have been accompanied by a number of general initiatives, culminating in the establishment of a police agency dedicated to protecting children from online sexual abuse (the Child Exploitation and Online Protection Centre). Most recently, the Byron Review made a number of recommendations concerning limiting children's access to online risk whilst also increasing their 'resilience' to potentially harmful material.[5] In order to achieve these aims, a new UK Council on Child Internet Safety has been set up to improve industry regulation and provide better information and education via government, law enforcement, schools and children's services.

Yet despite these moves, the 'e-safety' agenda has attracted criticism. In particular, some groups argue that current debates over online safety and risk are alarmist in their representation of the dangers that children and young people are actually likely to encounter when using ICTs. These arguments are supported by the mixed conclusions of recent research studies of the reported levels of risk encountered by young people. On the one hand, some studies report relatively high levels of unsafe and inappropriate ICT use by children. For example, one recent survey of 1700 Belgian primary pupils reported:

> a high level of unsafe Internet use, such as chatting with unknown persons, sending personal information and photos, and by some children even meeting these persons whom they only know via the Internet. A high percentage of the pupils report being shocked by material found on the Internet.[6]

On the other hand, many other studies present actual instances of ICT-related risk as a less frequent occurrence. For instance, recent US research found that 9 per cent of 10–17-year-olds who used the internet reported being targets of online harassment.[7] Similarly, in terms of accidental exposure to undesirable material, the UK government's own cyber-safety research found that 'accidentally going on [adult] sites often is very low'.[8] A Europe-wide research project found that many of the risks could be described as being 'mundane' rather than 'spectacular'.[9] For example, experience of encountering online pornography or feeling threatened by possible encounters with paedophiles was reported as being extremely rare. Much more frequent were risks arising from uncertainties concerning the legal status of downloading online material, misconceptions of the nature of the internet, and difficulties in working out the proper function of basic tools such as search engines.

This lack of definite evidence has led to a growing sense among some academics and media commentators that, while we should not deny the real dangers that can exist in some exceptional circumstances, the relation between risk, danger and incidence of harm implied in much of the official e-safety rhetoric is 'genuinely tenuous'.[10] If nothing else, the gap between the risks implied within the official e-safety agenda and the apparently far lower incidence of risk found by studies of children's engagement with ICTs suggests that more discussion needs to take place between adults, children and young people.

Recognizing the need for a child-centred approach to understanding issues of e-safety in primary schools, we were able to use our questionnaires and discussions to examine the experiences and understandings of the primary pupils in our study with regard to issues of 'e-safety' and managing risk during their everyday use of ICTs. In particular, we were able to address the following questions in relation to the following questions:

- How did pupils understand and talk about issues of safety and risk with regard to ICTs?
- How did these understandings differ by gender, age and school attended?
- How did concerns with safety and risk influence pupils' engagement with ICTs?
- What implications are there for the ongoing 'e-safety' agenda in schools and home?

We address these questions through two of the research methods outlined in Chapter 3 – our survey of 612 pupils, and the follow-up group discussions with 131 of these pupils. In both stages of the project we were able to ask a number of specifically focused questions, including pupils' perceptions of risk and suggestions for ensuring safe uses of ICTs.

Findings from our survey of pupils

It is worthwhile confirming from the outset that all five of our study schools took the topic of e-safety seriously. As Table 7.1 shows, all the schools were addressing the government guidelines and recommendations.

Table 7.1 Description of study schools' e-safety provision.

A: London inner city	E-safety provision included: formal e-safety policy with regard to appropriate use; assigned teacher as internet safety co-ordinator; classroom discussions on e-safety and safe searching.
B: London suburban	E-safety provision included: formal e-safety policy with regard to appropriate use; assigned teacher as internet safety co-ordinator; lessons delivered on ICT safety in ICT suite; e-safety posters in ICT suite.
C: West Midlands small town	E-safety provision included: formal e-safety policy with regard to appropriate use; assigned teacher as internet safety co-ordinator; classroom discussions on e-safety and safe searching.
D: London suburban	E-safety provision included: formal e-safety policy with regard to appropriate use; assigned teacher as internet safety co-ordinator; classroom discussions on e-safety and safe searching; pupils produced e-safety posters around classroom computers.
E: London inner city	E-safety provision included: formal e-safety policy with regard to appropriate use; assigned teacher as internet safety co-ordinator; lessons delivered on ICT safety in ICT suite; e-safety posters in ICT suite.

At first glance, most of the pupils in our study schools reported being knowledgeable about the risks of ICT use, and being able to avoid such risks. In our survey nearly three-quarters of pupils indicated that they had thought about how to avoid risks and dangers when using ICTs, with nearly all of these pupils also claiming to be aware of ways they could keep themselves safe when using computers, the internet and mobile phones (see Table 7.2).

However, when we asked pupils to provide examples of ways of being safe, only one-third were able to provide responses that corresponded to the official notions of e-safety outlined earlier. Invalid answers included keeping water away from the keyboard, keeping doors closed, not tripping over power cables and – in four responses – not using a computer at all. As can be seen in Table 7.2, the likelihood of pupils being able to give valid responses increased with age and frequency of ICT use. Responses also differed according to school attended, with pupils at the small town school C displaying higher levels of affirmation than those attending suburban or inner-city schools.

Table 7.2 Pupils' responses to questionnaire items concerning e-safety (percentages of pupils)

	Thought about risks and dangers of ICT use	Claimed to be aware of ways to avoid risks and dangers	Able to cite examples in line with official criteria
School			
A: London inner city	63	59	24
B: London suburban	63	66	46
C: West Midlands small town	83	81	46
D: London suburban	72	67	33
E: London inner city	77	73	24
Gender			
Male	69	70	31
Female	74	67	38
Year group			
3	79	58	11
4	72	73	22
5	67	64	37
6	72	74	46
TOTAL	**72**	**69**	**34**

A second section of the survey sought suggestions for improving ICT provision at school. As can be seen in Figure 7.1, pupils' views on potential improvements to school ICT provision highlighted a particular desire for increased assistance with internet safety, with safety-related issues being the first and fourth most popular improvements. This demand was especially prevalent from younger pupils and those who made relatively little use of ICTs in school.

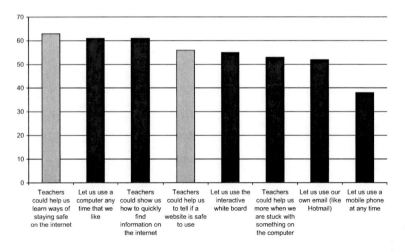

Figure 7.1 Pupils' views of improvements to teachers and teaching practice (data are percentages of pupils).

Findings from our pupil discussions

In line with these survey findings, many of the discussions also suggested that pupils' understandings and experiences of ICT-related risk often differed from the official 'e-safety' criteria. For instance, the majority of 'risky' or 'dangerous' issues that children reported concerned what can be best described as routine logistical or operational aspects of ICT use. These ordinary and mundane risks stood in marked contrast to the rather more extreme risks highlighted in the official definitions of e-safety. For instance, no pupils reported inappropriate contact with adults and only a few reported coming across 'rude' material. Pupils were most likely to relate the 'risks' of deleting documents, losing their place within games, getting into trouble with parents through mishandling error messages on the computer and, most commonly, the underlying risk of getting bored when playing games or using the internet. As we saw in Chapter 5, the dangers associated with ICT use were perhaps more accurately described as mishaps.

POINT TO CONSIDER

Dealing with pupils' ICT frustrations

For many pupils the 'dangers' of ICT use were described as involving deleting files, computers crashing or not functioning as expected. While such responses highlight these pupils' lack of direct experience of 'serious' risk or danger, they also highlight the many operational frustrations that children can experience when using computers. It is tempting to assume that all the children in your class are reasonably adept at using ICT. Yet if you take the time to see computer use from a child's perspective then some simple ways of improving classroom ICT may present themselves.

For instance, if you have time at the end of the day, ask all your pupils to do the following tasks:

- 'list five things that go wrong when using the computer'
- 'list things that annoy you when using the computers'

Common responses are likely to include words being blocked by internet filters, the difficulty of using a QWERTY keyboard or an adult-sized mouse, or not being able to see the screen in the sunlight. Often these annoyances can be alleviated or avoided altogether.

You can then discuss briefly any practical changes or adjustments that can be made to make things better.

In contrast, children's views of the *potential* risks of using ICTs – as opposed to incidents that they had actually experienced – were often exaggerated and, in some cases, verged on the fantastical. Most potential risks were based around extreme fears of having houses burgled through disclosure of personal information, being spied upon from hidden cameras, getting injured from hardware breaking, and, perhaps most imaginatively, the health risks of close contact to hardware. As one girl told us, 'Don't have [children] get too close to it because they'll get sterilized' (girl, Year 3, School C). It was clear that some of these perceived risks took the form of reconstructed news stories, folk-tale and urban myths. As these boys told us in one of the inner-city schools:

Boy1:   Once my cousin's friend he had a mobile in his hand and he was in a park and he got murdered ... this person murdered him to take the mobile off of him.

Int: *Actually murdered him?*

Boy1:   Yeah ... so that's not that safe.

Int: *They just killed him and took the phone? Is that near here?*

Boy1:   [pause] … No it as kind of far away

Girl: There could be dangerous stuff like if you're talking to someone while it's raining the electricity from the phone and the water from the rain if it touches electricity then you could get electrocuted.

Boy2:   On the news it was showing that there was a big murder … but no one murdered anyone, it was just that this boy … it was properly heavily raining that's why we didn't have no school, and this boy who was going out with a phone and he was playing games. And while he was in the Highfield Park while rain fell on the phone and he put it in his pocket and the next ten minutes he got electrocuted. And someone was cleaning up the rubbish on that rainy day and they saw him and called the police and everyone was showing it on the news.

Int: *I must have missed that.…*

Boy2:   It's dangerous if it's like lightening and that it's dangerous to do the iPods or the Nintendo Wii

Boy1:   And the electrical devices.

Int: *In a storm, a thunderstorm?*

Boy2:   Yeah otherwise the lightening might strike on it and you might …

Boy1:   and you get electrocuted while you're doing something

(Year 6, School E)

Pupils' accounts and descriptions tended to correspond with official notions of e-safety only in the case of recurring concerns over age appropriateness. Here we found high levels of anxiety about children seeing sites which were 'too old' for them. During many of the discussions, children were keen to highlight specifically 'rude' or violent websites that they were afraid would upset them. As this Year 3 boy argued:

Boy: Because certain websites are for adults not for children and if [children] went on that it might be a bit violent or get violent.

(Year 3, School D)

Interestingly, pupils only rarely expressed fears concerning the dangers of inappropriate contact through disclosure of personal information on websites. Of course, it could well be that children found these ideas either difficult to express, or that their understandings of these threats was underdeveloped. As this Year 4 boy considers:

Boy: You could bring them home, take them upstairs, show them the bedroom, they might steal you, they might put you in a bag and walk out.

(Year 4, School A)

The potential for misunderstanding can be seen in the following discussion of posting pictures online amongst Year 6 pupils. It seems that the girl in this interview group may have developed more sophisticated understandings:

Girl: I went once to put my pictures all up on a website and [interrupted voices over]
Boy1: ...they know what you look like.
Boy2: Because they might change your picture
Int: *Why?*
Girl: Because it's not really safe.
Int: *That's true.*
Boy1: They can look at you and know who you are.
Int: *They know your face...*
Girl: They could see you in the street one day and they might know you.
Boy2: They might take a picture of you and they might humiliate you with clown ears, red nose and green hair.

(Year 6, School B)

Given the vague nature of these responses, we were surprised to find that many of the children voiced exaggerated protectionist responses towards the need to regulate ICT use in school (although not necessarily their own ICT use). For instance, despite its popularity, some pupils were keen to have *YouTube* blocked in school:

Girl1: We're not allowed to use it but people secretly use it and we want it to be blocked.
Girl2: Yeah they privately use it so if it's blocked they can't use it.
Boy: Yeah.
Int: *Hang on a minute, so what you're saying is that people use YouTube secretly...?*
Boy: Yeah.
Int: *...and you would prefer it to be blocked so that they couldn't do that?*
Girl1: When they use it in secret they go on rude stuff and then sometimes when the teacher's working with other children,

when they're stuck, they just go on it and we don't want that
to happen, they look at rude things.

Boy: ...the little children they're going to grow up to be like that.

(Year 4, School E)

Other such 'improvements' to be made to ICTs were suggested throughout the interviews, such as the classification of age-appropriate websites, demanding that the 'makers' of *YouTube* be more selective and 'responsible' when accepting videos, password protection to be imposed on particular websites and, in one rather extreme suggestion, 'in every computer you could just delete *Google*' (boy, Year 4, School A).

The need to improve pupils' sense of e-safety

Although the pupils in our study seemed to recognize the need to be aware of ICT- related risks and dangers, the results from our survey and discussions also highlight some contradictions between the current official emphasis on 'e-safety' in schools and the experiences and understandings of primary pupils. On one hand, many of the children in our study clearly saw e-safety as an important issue that they thought needed addressing in schools. Indeed, the majority of pupils – especially those who were younger and less frequent users of ICT – were keen to highlight the need for more e-safety related practice within their schools. Yet the nature of most children's actual experiences of risk could be classed as rather prosaic and mundane inconveniences rather than dangers or risks.

In this sense, our discussions suggest that children's conceptions and actual experiences of e-safety were far removed from the e-safety agenda. Yet despite a lack of direct experience, many children still expressed exaggerated fears of the potential risks associated with ICT use that lacked clear understandings of the ICT-related risks that they are most likely to encounter, such as cyber-bullying and violent games. It is reasonable to conclude that e-safety, in the minds of the pupils in our study at least, remained an abstract and poorly understood concept.

POINT TO CONSIDER

Making it easier for pupils to talk about e-safety

It is often easier for pupils to talk about ICT risks and dangers in terms of people other than themselves. For instance, ask your pupils to design a leaflet about internet risks and dangers for children in the year group below them. Once you have got children to identify some things that they consider to be 'dangers' you can then discuss why these things are dangerous – who is in danger, and what might happen as a result. Although it may take some time, see if children can distinguish their suggestions in terms of the following categories:

- a realistic danger – 'this could happen to me';
- a remote danger – 'this could not happen to me';
- not really a danger at all – 'this is something that is annoying, but is not going to harm me or anyone else'.

It could be concluded that the children in our study were not especially 'risk-savvy'. Yet if we approach this topic from the perspective of the child (rather than from the concerns of the policy-makers and practitioners), then it could be argued that our findings merely reflect children's pragmatic and understandable responses to an adult issue that is itself vague and unclear. On the one hand, some of our pupils were certainly using ICTs as a focus for repeating general messages of risk and folk-stories about imagined 'danger'. On the other hand, many children were offering more immediate definitions of safety from the perspective of their own use of ICTs. This explains the accounts in which they do not encounter paedophiles, but instead trip over power cables, spill water on keyboards and accidently delete files.

We would contend that these responses are not necessarily incorrect or uninformed, but simply personal understandings of the risks, dangers and issues of safety from the perspective of the child's own experiences. The range and scope of responses to ICT use highlighted in this chapter would therefore suggest that popular perceptions of children as either vulnerable innocents or digital deviants are as misleading as they are alarming. We found little evidence in our study that children were either as uninformed *or* as competent about ICT safety matters as some adults fear. Instead our study suggests that the ongoing 'e-safety' agenda in schools requires rethinking and repositioning in ways that reflect what *does* happen and what *could* happen to children when using ICTs.

In other words, we would conclude that children's attention needs to be more effectively refocused away from the extremes of both the exceptional and the everyday 'risks' of ICT use, and towards the range of more 'intermediate' risks that are possible, rather than extremely likely or extremely unlikely. While these intermediate risks (cyber-bullying, accessing inappropriate content and so on) are undoubtedly part of the schools' e-safety provision, it would seem that such messages were not being taken on board by the pupils in our study as well as they could have been.

So, it seems clear that improvements can and should be made to how schools engage pupils with ICT risk and safety issues. It seems especially appropriate that schools discuss the topic of e-safety with pupils in ways that are meaningful and relevant to their actual experiences of ICT engagement. We discuss some ways that children can be encouraged to talk about ICT and develop a 'critical digital literacy' in Chapter 9. In the meantime, the next chapter goes on to discuss what the teachers, school leaders and the ICT co-ordinators from our study schools had to say about what we found in their schools and from their pupils.

8 Teachers learning from pupil perspectives?

Overview: This final empirical chapter in the book presents teachers' perspectives on the issues raised so far. It draws on our follow-up discussions with senior management teams, classroom teachers and ICT co-ordinators in the five study schools. In these discussions, teachers offer their thoughts and views on what their pupils told us about ICTs. Their reactions highlight some of the wider issues and organizational concerns that underlie the study's findings. The teachers also assess the practicalities of pupils' suggestions for change. The chapter concludes by identifying a number of areas where the demands of pupils may be best reconciled with the concerns and needs of schools. It also suggests areas of change that will *not* work.

Introduction

Up until now we have stressed the importance of listening carefully to what pupils have to say about ICTs. The previous four chapters have deliberately focused on children's views, experiences, opinions and accounts of ICT in primary schools. Unlike other books on primary ICT, we have put these concerns above those of teachers, school leaders and parents. Yet in emphasizing the need to listen to children about ICT we are not ignoring completely the need to consider the views of teachers and schools. We realize that it would be unwise to take everything that the children have said so far in the book at face value. Listening only to children without also allowing adults to have *their* say would provide only a partial account of primary ICT.

Any teacher or school leader would undoubtedly find much to agree *and* disagree with over Chapters 4–7. Whilst we were collecting the data we would often imagine how the schools' teachers would have responded to the views of their pupils if they had been there. Of course, part of the reason for allowing the children in our study to talk freely away from the presence of their teachers was to highlight the uncertainties and contestable areas of ICT use. Yet in allowing pupils to express their 'learner voice' we are not assuming that everything that was said should be 'taken as gospel' and followed unconditionally. Instead, we believe that pupil perspectives should be listened to, taken on board, and considered as part of the wider negotiation of how ICTs are used (and not used) within the primary school.

So, as the book nears its conclusion, it makes sense to ask classroom teachers, ICT co-ordinators and school leaders for their reactions to our findings. After all, most of our eventual suggestions for improving primary ICT will involve the co-operation of whole school communities. More importantly, teachers can provide a dose of realism on some of the more high-minded and idealistic issues raised so far. It is important to remember that the pupils in our study are not often concerned with fulfilling national curriculum objectives, balancing budgets, liaising with local authorities or dealing with governors. It is clear that our findings need to be set against the institutional 'realities' of primary education if they are to be of any practical use.

With these thoughts in mind, we waited for a few months after finishing our fieldwork in the five schools and then spent time analysing the data and drawing some tentative conclusions. After this break we returned to talk over our emerging 'findings' with the pupils' teachers, head teachers and ICT co-ordinators. We were certain that if we were to make the best use of our data then we needed to consider the institutional perspective on any improve-ments and adjustments we were thinking of suggesting. We were looking forward to having our ideas and suggestions challenged and rejected – taking the view that in order to make something work better, you first have to think of all the reasons why it might not work. In this spirit, the remainder of this chapter presents the 'teacher voice' on primary ICT in the five study schools.

Talking with teachers about technology

Teachers are used to hearing things from children that are uncomfortable and sometimes critical. Conversations between teachers and children take place in primary schools all day long – in classrooms, dining halls, playgrounds and even ICT suites. Yet wherever and whenever teachers get to talk with pupils, these conversations almost always take place on an unequal footing. There are clear power differences between the different roles of 'teacher' and 'pupil'. This inevitably means that when a teacher asks an opinion of a child in school, the child can feel obliged to give the answer that she thinks the teacher would like to hear. This power imbalance exists however carefully teachers choose their words to elicit honest and authentic opinions from children. It is rare that pupils and teachers say exactly what they think to each other.

The teachers in our study had joined our research project in the full knowledge that they might hear things that they did not expect, or even want, to hear from their pupils about ICT. In the event, teachers almost always reacted to our findings in an even-handed and positive manner. Only on a couple of occasions were teachers indignant or dismissive of what they heard. This is not to say that there was no disagreement or frustration with what was said by pupils – yet on the whole, teachers were intrigued to be hearing things from the children in their school through an independent source. All the staff had taken part in the study in order to learn and to open up connections with their pupils, so most welcomed the opportunity to hear from their pupils in a different way.

Our follow-up discussions with staff focused on the content of our official end-of-project report. The schools had all received copies of the project summary a few weeks before we returned to talk with them, and it was clear that some had already used the outcomes as a basis for some fairly significant discussions and decisions. These were concerned mainly with issues of management, resource allocation and proposals to external bodies for funding. Most of the schools were also interested in the possibilities for training that enabled staff to learn more about 'freeing up' the curriculum and finding out more about the creative aspects of ICT use. Yet besides these initial responses, many of the teachers and managers were keen to discuss specific local issues and constraints that they saw as central to the prospect of making future progress with ICT in their schools. It is these issues that will be most useful for our final recommendations and conclusions.

The remainder of this chapter focuses on teachers' responses across the study schools – highlighting seven key themes that emerged from our discussions. This is followed by a summary of what teachers thought could realistically be done to move things forward with regard to ICT use in their school (as well as what they thought could not work). The seven key themes that emerged in the teacher responses were as follows:

- recognizing differences between school culture and home culture;
- matters of staff development and training;
- the pressures of meeting national policy and local authority demands;
- the place of ICT in primary curriculum reform and change;
- parental expectations;
- 'e-safety' and 'appropriate use';
- the pressures of involving pupils in school decision-making.

Recognizing differences between school culture and home culture

There was widespread acknowledgement during our discussions that teachers often had little idea of what some of their pupils were using ICT for. Even some ICT co-ordinators admitted that our project had introduced them to an unfamiliar range of ICT applications. In many ways this is to be expected – applications such as *Neopets*, *Club Penguin* and *Stardoll* are aimed solely at a 'tween' audience of primary-age children. It would perhaps have been more surprising if the teachers had demonstrated a close working knowledge of these applications. Yet it was clear that many teachers were unfamiliar with the general types of applications their pupils were using. Many teachers struggled to draw parallels between the children's uses of ICT and their own experiences – most having no knowledge of similar adult-focused activities or applications such as multiplayer online games, social networking sites and virtual worlds.

These gaps in knowledge and experience pointed to a wider gap between how often adults talk about ICT and the use they make of it. Despite all the current talk in educational circles of web 2.0 applications, the number of primary teachers who keep active *Facebook* profiles, who maintain a *Twitter* feed or who visit virtual worlds such as *Second Life* is small. So it is unrealistic to expect teachers to have an empathy with the 'tween' versions of these activities. This gap did mean that most teachers in our discussion groups were genuinely surprised at what children could use these sites for – especially the communal, communicative and creative aspects of most sites such as *Habbo*, *Neopets* or *CBeebies*. Over the course of our discussions it was therefore possible for the teachers to quickly pick out useful sets of skills and dispositions which some children clearly were exhibiting through their use of these applications that were certainly not being assimilated into the life of the classroom.

In this sense there was evident awareness of the cultural gap between some children's home experiences of technologies and their school-based experiences. In many cases, teachers expressed the necessity of learning more about children's digital cultures. As one senior manager in School A reflected:

> I mean we haven't got a clue about [such sites]. I mean that's possibly where we need to learn from them and also it'll be interesting to see what they're doing at home because I mean … we get a view on their home life, and what dominates… what's consistent is the screen. So you wonder, what are they watching?

The idea that all partners in the learning process could learn from each other was imagined differently in another school. Here it was suggested that the school should act as a place where models of 'best practice' could be provided for children to then take back into their home use of ICT. As one teacher suggested:

> what they do at home, and how what we do at school is sometimes so completely different, it needs to go both ways. I would like to see that they're liking *Excel* in school and that it's also going home now…
>
> (School B)

It was telling that this teacher used the example of the *Excel* spreadsheet application – despite our findings of the relative unpopularity of spreadsheet use amongst her pupils. Nevertheless, she described how she already provided ideas to encourage pupils to try using spreadsheets at home and was pleased to feel that a two-way exchange was taking place between her and her pupils:

> Year 5 is what I have, and we're doing spreadsheets at the moment, and I try to make it interesting for them, and I said to them, who has a computer at home? Who has *Microsoft Office*, who has *Excel*? And they're all like 'oh, it's that green X, but they've never used it'. And so they want to now go and try and do the things that we've tried at school at home. So I think sometimes school needs to introduce something so that they can try and find out what it's about, otherwise they would never have touched it.
>
> (School B)

Other teachers were more circumspect about the obvious home–school divide in children's ICT use and ICT interest. As the head teacher from School C reasoned:

> No, that doesn't surprise me. I mean you'd expect them to like the games better wouldn't you, really?

For some teachers our findings simply reflected the 'directed' realities of schools and the more 'personal' realities of children's home lives. Put simply, school and home were accepted to be very different places, fulfilling very different roles in very different ways, as the head teacher commented:

> Yeah, I think computers outside of the home are for fun, and they are very personal, aren't they? It's for me to do what I want to do, for me to be able to chat to people I want to chat to, send messages, look at pictures, play games and look at things. And whereas in school it's directed and I'm doing the same as other people, maybe, and it doesn't feel so individual.
>
> (School C)

Teachers made this distinction between home choices and school coercion across all of our discussions. Crucially, though, many teachers recognized that 'non-directed' was not necessarily the same as 'of little value'. Most teachers could see the educational potential of children's more time-consuming but 'looser' ICT activities at home that had a potential for productive and creative activity. Our discussions in one school, for example, centred on their use of digital photography with children. We asked if children's activities in popular photo-sharing applications such as *Flickr* could be continued at school, having been begun outside. The head teacher in School C responded positively to the general idea but also sounded a cautious note with respect to the technological difficulties inherent in such a home/school 'transfer':

> this is something we're working towards with the learning platform again, really, a sharing of things that maybe I've done at home, or maybe that I've done at school I can share with home. But it's the technology, again, that can get in the way. This is why you tend to stick with *Office* really for things. Sad, isn't it? But it's things that parents have got, so it has to be that way.

Other teachers expressed the view that, whilst there may well be some value in allowing children to work with their 'home' ICTs in school settings, in practice there were considerable resource implications for parents or for schools which often would overshadow any potential pedagogical advantages:

> maybe there's a line [between home and school], in which case some things that children do at home can enhance their learning in school, it doesn't necessarily mean that you need to be doing school stuff in the home, and I don't think it would be a good use of money for us to buy class sets of *Nintendo*'s so they can all buy *Animal Paradise* when they're working on live processes and living things. That's just wrong …
>
> (School D)

As the quotation above suggests, by far the most significant element of children's home ICT culture was recognized to be the use of computer games and games consoles. Teachers were unsurprised by the high levels of use and interest in games that were apparent in our study. Whilst many were sceptical of the educational value of computer games, some schools were receptive to the newer genres of brain-training and fitness games. After conceding that the choices of the 'newest' and 'best' games on the market would always win over any educationally-orientated titles, the head teacher in School C commented on the positive effects of some popular games consoles:

> I think I would always expect children to go for game and game technology… I think there is a place for the *Wii*, actually, in terms of physical activity and as a motivational tool for those children who are not so keen on physical activity. I mean, I think that would be quite good, actually, it's like the old dance mats and things, isn't it?

It would seem from these discussions that our confirmation of differences between children's use of technology at home and their experiences at school was not news to any of the teachers. However, the ways in which the teachers then went on and conceived being able to 'work with' children's home uses of ICT (rather than simply ignoring them) was interesting. Although many were aware of children's ICT interests and skills, most teachers did not feel fully competent and confident to reach across the divide and make use of these interests and skills in the classroom. Children's home use was certainly not an unknown quantity, but was not known enough to be made full use of in the classroom.

Matters of staff development and training

Many of the teachers and senior managers in the study schools saw our findings as indicating the need for additional staff training and development. Turning to training to address perceived shortcomings is a common response in education. Training is a clear way to demonstrate that a school is taking an issue seriously – especially in the eyes of external groups such as school inspectors and parents. Yet in this instance, schools' keenness for extra training also reflected a genuine desire to learn more about a topic that they recognized they were not competent in. One head teacher spoke of using training to reverse the effects of 'the fear factor' amongst his staff:

> Then we have ... a vast difference in some of the levels of knowledge, and there's a fear factor for those [teachers] that are not comfortable and confident, because as things are dramatically changing now, they're getting a little bit more freaked out. And actually, all we want to do is to set up a situation where we're just supporting them and saying it's not as bad as you think...
>
> (School A)

In particular, schools highlighted the need for training that introduced teachers to ICTs they otherwise would be unfamiliar with, and then reflected on the potential for learning gains if used in the classroom. The same head teacher described her experiences of playing computer games with her children, which she had attempted to feed back into her own teaching and conducting of assemblies:

> I was thinking ... 'what is it about this that? What elements of this could come into a playful situation in school?' So I'm asking myself the question more about how to use these things for myself. Plus film, attaching pictures and presenting in assemblies and all those sorts of things.
>
> (School A)

In the eyes of another head teacher, training was also required to aid the use of 'teacher-led' technologies in ways that were inspired by children's ways of using 'their' own technologies. She singled out the interactive whiteboard as something that was generally welcomed in her school as an ICT that was under the teacher's control yet also appeared to pupils as innovative and engaging. The head teacher described that her teachers' initial use of whiteboards had resembled their previous use of blackboards, with teachers feeling most confident to lead class discussion from the front. Only when teachers had gained confidence to use the technology with their pupils had more expansive forms of use occurred:

> because when they came in, in the early days, and IT was a bit scary for staff, then give them the tool that is quite familiar. I can teach from the front with a familiar type of system here, that was great, and that worked really well. And then the next stage was, well, did you realize, actually, it's even better when you get the children to interact with them, and that was coming through on performance management and all kinds of things. So we've had quite a push on getting children to interact within and working with groups on them.
>
> (School C)

Underlying our discussions with staff in the five schools was a feeling that schools first needed to make an effort to help teachers see children's ICT activities as something that could become part of their own 'comfort zones', before then looking at ways of teachers integrating these ICTs into their own teaching practice. This two-stage process of comfortableness followed by use required ongoing training and development.

The pressures of meeting national policy and local authority demands

Many of our discussions moved quickly to matters of school organization and administration. For most school leaders, any ambition to expand ICT use throughout school communities came second to more pressing concerns of resourcing and procurement strategies and the balancing of school finances. As the head teacher at School A acknowledged, there had simply not been sufficient time for her school to consider any of the points that our research report raised about their school:

> To be honest, we haven't taken it further into the staff conversation yet, because, rather than focusing on curriculum development within the ICT, we'd be very much looking at how to organize the budget.

Similarly, other schools also reported finding that pressures around staffing and human resources outweighed the priorities of ICT innovation and change. As the head teacher at School C put it:

> It's the management costs of it which are highly influential for us. We can look at capital costs of buying things in, but it's the management of the stuff that really, really costs.

As outlined in Chapter 1, primary ICT is set against some 'big' priorities and pressures that have little to do with pupils' learning. Here, too, teachers contrasted the findings from our study against a range of ways in which they were held accountable. These checks and balances included external official inspections, local authority guidelines, equipment suppliers and national agencies such as Becta and the Department for Children, Schools and Families (DCSF). Head teachers were keen to stress their relative lack of autonomy in determining the state of ICT within their schools – highlighting a variety of outside pressures that often had a blocking effect on our suggestions for change or adjustment. These included financial constraints, limits on suppliers, curriculum pressures and resource implications.

The five schools in our study were situated in three different local authorities. The guidance given to schools on ICT differed between each authority, with varying degrees of central control. One local authority had retained control of all budgeting and ICT procurement decisions, whilst another had devolved decision-making to schools in nearly all areas of ICT. That said, all the schools in our study reported local authorities as exerting some influence over what they could and could not do with ICT. This was evident, for example, in the case of one school that had attempted an innovative use of games consoles of the kind envisaged by the children in the project. Despite taking place many years before, the discouraging advice of one ICT adviser from the local authority had been retained as part of the schools' institutional memory, as one teacher related:

> We got told off a few years ago. Actually in about 2000 I was doing 'instructions' in Literacy for the children, it was a Year 4 class, but we used a *Game Boy*, the big, old grey *Game Boy*, because that was all there was at that time, how you use it, you switch it on, you put the ...
> And they could do it, because they liked being able to have the *Game Boy* in school, and it was the adviser who said that's not ICT. I said, but

> this isn't an ICT display, it's a Literacy display and it's instructions, and
> just because you're seeing the *Game Boy*, I'm not saying that that was
> ICT, we were doing it for how you use it. But they didn't want to have
> that cross-over with games consoles and computers.
>
> (School B)

Past incidents such as these had a profound bearing on the ways that schools approached ICT, with teachers in this particular school wary of using games consoles in the future. Such advice was not coming solely from local authority staff. Curriculum advisory teams were not in place across all authorities and in some schools had been replaced by IT industry staff who only supported products which were sold through the company. This was seen as further reducing autonomy on the part of the school. As the head teacher at School C put it:

> there were the curriculum leaders as well who would come in from
> [company name], because our old advisory teachers lost their jobs
> and were re-employed by [company name]. So they came into
> schools to support the packages that we [bought], so we get better
> pricing structures for the software and things like that.

These local influences were accompanied by a variety of other bodies seeking to influence and shape primary ICT. This combination of local and national pressures was apparent, for example, in one school's intentions to implement the kinds of 'personalized' ICT use recommended by the government's Harnessing Technology strategy through the use of *Moodle* – an open-source managed learning environment. These plans were stymied by the restrictions of an authority-wide procurement contract and other localized arrangements for ICT that the school were obliged to adhere to. In such cases, meeting some of the kinds of changes suggested by the children in earlier chapters was simply not possible. How ICT was being used in some schools was often based around commercial rather than educational priorities. As another head teacher put it:

> Now, if you take what's happening ...we are driven by the *Building
> Schools for the Future* programme – £10million in [borough] which is
> the IT bit to have a menu service. Now, once you get a menu service,
> [name] is one that contracts across the local area, like it or not, the
> learning platform which they are supporting and promoting of that
> managed package is [name]. ... So in other words, you have no way of
> getting a new infrastructure sorted out for your IT stuff. ... The

government's wish to have a central database that works and talks to one another through DCSF is a million miles away, because each authority, when you talk to these people, is already working in isolation. Very few are working together.

(School E)

The place of ICT in primary curriculum reform and change

Besides these national and local external pressures, all the schools in our study were also wary of the changing place of ICT in the primary curriculum and the imminent demands of the curriculum changes proposed in the Independent Primary Review led by Sir James Rose (see Chapter 1). Despite not being due to be introduced until 2011, these reforms were already having an effect on teachers' thinking about ICT. One teacher looked up from reading our research report summary and, in response to the various findings, reflected:

we need to reconsider and move away from the idea that ICT is a subject and be more cross-curricular, and look at it more that it's actually behind what's going on, it's everywhere. It's not 'now it's time to go into the ICT suite for one hour a week and that's the end of it', that's not what we want to see happening.

(School A)

Clearly what had struck him from our findings was the need to respond to children's pleas for greater freedom of ICT access and use – especially in terms of the time allocated to ICT and the spaces within the curriculum for ICT use. This sense of moving away from delivering ICT as a subject and towards a different model of envisaging ICT as something around which to build other subject experiences was echoed by other teachers. As the head teacher at School C argued:

My view is that I wish, like all the subjects, actually, that they would have written a progression of skills, because it's the skills that they use within the context of other things that's important. So general progression of skills – and technology's moved on such a lot since the National Curriculum was written anyway, the types of experiences that they should be having, so that you can start looking and mapping them more carefully across the curriculum.

These teachers and others were therefore anticipating shifts in UK primary education towards more cross-curricular work with ICT. As this head teacher went on to say:

> I'm waiting for the Rose Review which I know is going to say: 'so in the primary school – cross-curricular then'. And it's still going to be up to us to decide curriculum, which is fine, but we could use it as an opportunity for using media ... all that sort of stuff.
>
> (School C)

This quotation acknowledges an emerging pressure on schools to go beyond focusing teacher efforts on getting children to use technology and develop what could be called 'functional sets' of ICT skills. Indeed, teachers often reflected on their dissatisfaction with the current curriculum arrangements and how they limited the uses of ICTs in school. As one teacher in School A complained, there was a sense that planning for ICT was an additional burden not accounted for in the existing primary curriculum strategies:

> Well, I know ... that through the sort of dominating English and Literacy planning that the two PCs that exist in the classroom are really hard to plan into that time. And that is, if you like, almost half the day, and that, I think, is a problem. And if it's difficult to plan two PCs into Literacy and Numeracy sessions ...

Parental expectations

Parents were mentioned in our discussions with teachers in two main ways – in a partnership role but also in an occasionally adversarial sense, especially with respect to issues of e-safety. In terms of using ICT as a focus for developing partnerships with parents, one school described their attempts to build activities around ICT into their 'family learning' programme. The head teacher in School E explained that his school was aiming to empower parents without the time or resources to engage fully with ICTs on their own:

> and that's why we do the Family Learning thing. Because I would say probably the majority of our parents aren't computer literate, are they, when it comes down to it? In honesty. They'll say oh, yeah, I can use *Word*. They'll come in and if you're doing some little thing, you see them looking and watching, and the next thing – I don't want to do this wrong, what do I do to turn it on? This computer's different to

mine, you know. Just simple things like that. So what we're trying to do is work with parents to empower them.

The same head teacher also talked of training parents in ICT skills and encouraging them to engage with their children's ICT use. In this school at least, a programme of parental ICT training was being considered through the mechanisms of clubs and family learning groups. This was said to be a clear priority in the school plan and the school was determined to place it at the centre of activities:

> We know what we want to do and where we want to go, it's just how we're gonna get there. Now, a number of those elements of what you talked about, tying up school and tying up home and tying in parents is the very key thing we're doing across the board.
>
> (School E)

Other schools, however, acknowledged a general lack of parental interest in improving the state of educational ICT in their school. Some head teachers saw most parents – like their children – as having low expectations for school ICT use. In this case they had found parents to have come to expect there to be differences in ICT between school and home, as the head teacher at School D described:

> I mean, interestingly as well, we've had no real comments from parents about sort of ICT or thinking that the curriculum should be more twenty-first century, if you like, at all, and there doesn't seem to be any message coming from parents and carers in terms of the latest survey, which is suggesting that there's not a right balance. It seems to me that their perception is that that stuff is for home and this is how we do it in school and that's probably how it should be. And it doesn't really go on to explore [differences]…

'E-safety' and 'appropriate use'

One area of school ICT where parents were reported to take an interest and exert pressure on schools, however, was that of e-safety and 'appropriate use' outlined in Chapters 1 and 7. In all of our five study schools, teachers recognized parental concern about e-safety. This was said to make teachers feel put into a position of heightened trust and responsibility. Like their pupils in Chapter 7, many of the teachers in the study schools were able to relate personal anecdotes about the risk and dangers of pupils' internet use. As the head teacher of School C described when dealing with a recent difficult e-safety situation in her school:

> So I thought, right, I'm gonna find out what's going on here, so I went in at home, when I could get access to *Bebo*, and it was just horrendous because they'd linked across to each other, they'd given passwords, they'd given addresses, they'd given phone numbers, they'd put photographs on, not of themselves, 'cos you're not supposed to do that, but their friends and their friends' friends, and their friends' families, all kinds of stuff.

The incident that this teacher described concerned an episode of cyber-bullying via the *Bebo* social networking site, involving a particularly vicious character assassination of an individual pupil by other members of their class. The parents had reacted furiously when the incidents came to light and, with the additional pressure of an impending external inspection, the school was required to take swift action. Two things emerged as a result. The first was the slow restoration of the trust of the parent body through the school being seen to take the incident seriously and act accordingly. Secondly, however, was the apparent withdrawal of pupils from wanting to talk with teachers about any aspects of their ICT use. As the head teacher went on to say:

> what we've noticed is since that incident and since all the work that we've done on e-safety, when you talk maybe within a circle time about it, the children … do not wish to share with you, honestly, what they've done, where they've been, and they'll shut down on you, because they're concerned that you're going to cut down their ICT use at home.
>
> (School C)

Teachers in other schools had also come across similar troubling incidents. One of these concerned a pupil in School B, as a teacher there explained:

> We had some Year 5s looking at pornography at home, in a child's bedroom. He had a loft conversion and his parents wouldn't come upstairs because the staircase was too rickety, and he was out of the way, and he'd hand his plates down after he'd finished, so he had his private den but was accessing this site that was found out about, because there's a mistake just there, and some older boys had told the

> boys go to this website. It's free, you can look at whatever you want.
> And the children were – they were horrified at what they had seen.
> And I thought that's you looking at it at home in the safety of your
> home, but very unsafe in your little den upstairs.

Incidents like this were used in the interviews to underline the fact that schools were continually acting to 'do the right thing' in terms of restricting and protecting children's ICT use. One teacher pointed to the productive safety discussions between pupils and teachers that had accompanied the recent creation of a new school website. This joint activity had allowed for the public airing of the potential risks of revealing identity and, therefore, created an atmosphere within School B in which the issues of e-safety had been given some thought:

> I mean they do need to be safe, and I suppose we've got our website
> now so they know about pictures and faces and names and things like
> that, so they're aware of that. But yeah, at the beginning of the year
> every teacher should go over those things, and talk about that it's not
> just at school where you need to be safe, it's at home, even more so.

After the incident in her school, the head teacher in School C reflected on events:

> I do think they have a genuine worry about staying safe on the
> internet. I do think they have a genuine concern about it. But the
> desire and the need to communicate out of school in that way is so
> great that it's pushed to one ... we're doing it, but we know that we
> might be doing something a little bit ooh-ooh, it's that kind of thing
> really. Because if you take – particularly when they get to 11 – if you
> take away their ability to communicate electronically out of school,
> you're chopping their hands off. It's like us, maybe as kids, not being
> allowed to telephone ... The days when you say I'm taking your
> computer away because you've done X, Y, Z wrong – woo! It's mega.
> Because you're chopping off a communication channel for them.

From this perspective, some schools were encouraging children to learn the skills of self-regulation and how to avoid being a victim or a perpetrator of inappropriate activity online. Teachers in schools that had not experienced recent incidents appeared to be more sanguine about these issues and concerns, recognizing the ease with which the school can become overwhelmed by messages of danger and protectionism. That said, all these teachers were aware that to slip up in any way would expose them to risk from regulatory bodies as well as from parents and press alike.

The pressures of involving pupils in school decision-making

A final major theme from our discussions concerned the growing sense from our data that decisions concerning the management of ICT in school could involve greater input from pupils. We were looking here to build upon the sense emerging from our pupil discussions and drawings where children had highlighted the restriction in school of having to ask permission to do things with ICT, as opposed to the more relaxed active and playful forms of ICT use they were used to outside school.

During our discussions with teachers and head teachers, several suggestions were offered that sought to increase the involvement of pupils in school decision-making. One suggestion that seemed to find broad agreement involved setting up pupil groups to discuss ICTs in school. It was suggested, for example, that these could be part of existing structures intended to support pupil democracy and participation in decision-making, such as school councils. It was also suggested that schools could encourage the formation of standalone groups around the uses of ICTs.

The responses of the teachers to these ideas were interesting. One school argued that such participatory groups were already in existence in the form of computer clubs and other non-statutory provision. The head teacher in School E saw ICT as potentially playing a part in their plans for an 'extended school' approach:

> Well, we've actually started to do that [involve pupils in decision-making], and we've started to do that through extended school, but not generally across the curriculum, because with the other pressures of what we have to do, there's not enough time to engage the whole class.

An ICT co-ordinator from School A responded positively to the suggestion but highlighted the need for support from the senior management team in trying to get this approach off the ground:

> It sounds to me like one of the follow-up things we could do would be to have this discussion group, a chaired discussion group around ICT, perhaps led by [the head teacher], which would take us forward.

> Because the pupil's voice is not going to get heard unless there is a
> sufficient facilitation of that follow-up report.

In School B our visit coincided with some of the pupils having
just approached their ICT co-ordinator to ask for a greater role in
the organizing of the school website. These proposals included an
idea for a dedicated online presence on the school website which
would better facilitate and amplify their role in the school
community and which they themselves would maintain:

> I have school council workers in my class and they're very into their
> job, and they came to me on Friday saying could we have a page on
> the website so that we can promote ourselves … And they wanted to
> know how to do it as well, so I'm sure there's an interest there.
>
> (School B)

In theory, then, greater learner input was an idea that all the
teachers expressed positive feelings towards – although practical
reservations remained over the time and resources required to
make such changes. Although the systems and pressures that
surround most schools may put a natural brake on increased pupil
involvement in management issues, many teachers were sympathetic to it as an aspiration, as this quotation from the head teacher
in School C illustrates:

> And I think you know, let's use the computer any time we like, yeah,
> I'm with that. I mean I would quite like them, and we work towards
> that at the top end of the school, I'm not saying we're there, but that's
> what we would like, so that they can say to us I think ICT would be a
> good tool for this…

What teachers thought would work and not work

We were pleased to be able to share our findings with the five
schools, and we were genuinely informed and enlightened by their
responses. Conversely, the classroom teachers, ICT co-ordinators
and head teachers appeared pleased to be able to hear from their
pupils through the project, acknowledging the value of the things
that they had learned. Perhaps most importantly, teachers were
able to give us a sense of what suggestions for change arising from
the project they felt could work. Conversely, they were also able to

highlight changes that might be more difficult to achieve amidst the organizational constraints of the primary school. In particular, teachers were able to identify the following issues that they could see as usefully informing future changes to their school ICT provision:

- ✓ Encouraging greater use of ICTs in other areas of the curriculum.
- ✓ Encouraging user groups, led by children, which could support resource allocation and feed into school-wide policies on ICT use.
- ✓ Establishing dialogue in the classroom about children's uses of ICTs at home and at school. Opening up channels of communication about children's use of games, social networking sites, search engines and so on.
- ✓ Encouraging more discussion in class about what it really means to be 'safe' when using ICTs and which were the techniques best suited to feeling secure online.
- ✓ Encouraging more discussion in class about information skills – e.g. what can be considered to be 'true' and 'trustworthy' on a website;

Conversely, though, doubts remained in areas where teachers felt that key factors were out of the immediate control of the school, namely:

- ✗ Any relaxation of rules that caused the school to be in breach of its duty of care at school. This would include the ability of schools to lift bans on certain websites (such as *YouTube* and *Flickr*).
- ✗ Any changes that entailed extra spending or contradicted contractual agreements or local authority guidance.
- ✗ Any changes that entailed neglecting the set curriculum or significantly increased staff time.
- ✗ Any changes that entailed breaches of security or increased risk of theft.

We can now take all these issues and viewpoints forward into our final chapter. Here we can attempt to identify the main issues underlying the state of ICT use in our study schools, and then make some practical suggestions on how to readjust and reconfigure primary schools as sites of innovative, imaginative and perhaps even empowering technology use for pupils and their teachers.

Suggestions for changing primary ICT

9

Overview: This chapter rounds off the book by using all of our findings from the research project to suggest ways of reconstituting primary schools as thriving sites of ICT use. We argue that schools should explore ways of relaxing restrictions on internet access and develop informed dialogues with children about ICT. In particular, the chapter highlights ways to develop 'cultures of trust' between pupils and schools with regard to their ICT use. The book concludes with a five-point agenda for change that, if implemented, could see schools revitalized as sites of informal, innovative and imaginative ICT use.

Introduction

The big question that always faces education researchers once having completed a research project is 'so what?'. So what do your findings mean for the real world? What useful conclusions can be offered to teachers, head teachers, policy-makers and other people concerned with primary education? This chapter concludes the book by addressing the 'so what?' question – outlining what we found and what we think it means. In particular, we draw together the important issues for primary schools that we feel have emerged from our research, and move towards making some recommendations and suggestions for change. As such, we use this chapter to answer a number of questions. How can we make sense of the complex and sometimes contradictory picture of primary ICT that our study has revealed? What options for changes, alterations and adjustments arise from our findings? What practical suggestions for teachers and schools can be given? Above all, we reconsider the overarching aim of our research project as set out in Chapter 3, namely:

- What lessons can be drawn from pupils' present experiences of using ICTs for formal and informal learning in terms of imagining new and different ways in which technology can be used in schools in the future?

With these thoughts in mind, the first section of this chapter reviews what we have found out about children's present experiences of ICT. In light of the previous five chapters of research findings, what do we know about how primary children actually make use of ICTs? How do these new understandings compare to the arguments, assumptions and assertions reviewed at the beginning of the book?

The digital native – myth and reality

The previous five chapters have revealed a rather ambiguous picture of children's uses of ICTs at school and home. The one immediate conclusion that springs to mind is that primary pupils are certainly not all high-tech 'digital natives' who are expert users and 'hard-wired' to work with ICT. That said, we certainly found technology at school and home to have a significant presence in the lives of primary pupils. Nearly all of the children in our study were certainly more comfortable with ICTs than their predecessors would have been even five years ago. The schools in our study were all making extensive efforts to provide their pupils with opportunities to make use of ICTs for learning. In short, ICT was an important part of the lives of many pupils. But we found little evidence to suggest that ICT was the most important part of their lives. The defining feature of the children in our study often seemed to be that they were children, not that they were technology users.

In fact we found primary pupils' actual uses of ICTs to be rather more limited in scope than many adult commentators would like to presume. Our survey found a predominance of games playing, chatting and communication, and looking at information and images on the internet. Younger children were also using computers for writing and making pictures. It is important to note that these 'high-tech' activities did not appear to be dominating or even damaging children's lives. These children were also watching a lot of television. Some were reading a lot of books. They were all coming to school. Nearly all were spending a lot of their time talking and playing with friends and taking part in family life. There were very few signs of children suffering from a 'toxic childhood' through overexposure and misuse of ICTs.

It seems to us that much of the hype currently surrounding ICT and primary-age children stems from the very high-profile technology habits and predilections of teenagers and young adults. It also seems that there is little evidence to suggest that what teenagers are assumed to be doing with ICTs is necessarily applicable to younger children. For example, in comparison to recent excitement over the apparently changing nature of children's internet use, our study found few instances of creative and collaborative uses of web 2.0 applications. When children were using web 2.0 tools such as *Habbo* or *YouTube*, the dominant use was for the passive consumption rather than active production of content. While some commentators may like to imagine collaborative communities of primary-age children involved in the creation and sharing of content, in reality most pupils' engagement with technology was far more passive, solitary, sporadic and unspectacular, both at home and at school.

This lack of sophistication was also evident with regard to children's sense of the risks and dangers associated with ICT use, especially when it came to the internet. Although most children were aware of the importance of 'e-safety', far fewer actually displayed any working knowledge of what this meant. In this sense, our findings echo recent studies of teenagers which also found a general 'lack of reflectiveness' regarding adult concerns over online risks, with concepts such as cyber-bullying either not recognized at all or else repeated second hand from news coverage and folk stories.[1]

Digital differences between children

Of course, we would not claim that our findings were applicable to every child in our study. There were distinct differences between different groups of children and schools, although perhaps not as consistently as we might have expected. For instance, although gender was not a significant difference in our survey data, there was evidence from the children's discussions that ICT remains different for boys and girls in a number of subtle ways. During the discussions, for example, children conveyed a strong sense of what ICT applications and activities they felt were appropriate for boys and girls, suggesting that gender stereotyping of activities such as computer games and online chatting remains prevalent. Girls were expected to play *Stardoll* and boys to play *Runescape*. ICT was not a site, at least for this age group, where gendered identities were being questioned or challenged.

Differences in pupils' ICT use were also found between the five schools in our study. The activities for which children were using ICTs, when and where they were doing them, and with what outcomes, all differed significantly between the five schools. As discussed at the end of Chapter 4, it is likely that these school differences relate to a number of factors, including the physical location of the computers within the school, the curricular organization of the school, the experience of the teachers, the type of learning environments beyond the schools, as well as the range and depth of support from local authorities. Nevertheless, there are so many factors at play here that it is impossible for us to identify any 'school effect'. All we can safely say is that differences between schools were apparent.

Above all, we found children's age group to be a significant influence on their ICT needs, interests and practices. As we saw in Chapter 4, activities such as making use of the internet for learning, along with database and spreadsheet use, increased as children grew older, whilst activities such as playing computer games, chatting, making pictures and using digital cameras all decreased. Older children were more likely to feel that they were learning from ICT use at school *and* home. Yet the findings from our survey and discussion sessions also highlighted the increased seriousness and the increased dulling of school ICT use as children progressed through Years 3–6. This importance of age is perhaps unsurprising. As any teacher or parent will know, the social, cultural and cognitive backgrounds of a 7-year-old child are very different from those of a 9-year-old. In turn, a 9-year-old has very different social, cultural and cognitive backgrounds than an 11-year-old. It seems that ICT use is heavily age-dependent even within the relatively limited age range of Key Stage 2. In this respect primary-age children's ICT use is no different than any other aspect of their growing up.

Gauging pupils' demands for change

Instead of finding evidence of a mounting 'digital disconnection' or disaffection between children and their schools, our research suggested a rather less fractious state of compliance. If anything, we found the children in our study to be relatively accepting of the rules, regulations and restrictions of their schools. Many of our pupils were distinctly circumspect and 'school-savvy' when it came to understanding what they could and could not do with ICT. They appeared to have learned to 'go with the flow' when necessary. While we certainly found evidence of disgruntlement, we also found a sense of pupils 'making the best of a bad lot'. From this perspective, public concerns over the alienated and angry 'digital native' may be rather wide of the mark. As Sue Bennett and colleagues argue:

> The picture beginning to emerge from research on young people's relationships with technology is much more complex than the digital native characterisation suggests. While technology is embedded in their lives, young people's use and skills are not uniform. There is no evidence of widespread and universal disaffection, or of a distinctly different learning style the like of which has never been seen before. We may live in a highly technologised world, but it is conceivable that it has become so through evolution, rather than revolution. Young people may do things differently, but there are no grounds to consider them alien to us. Education may be under challenge to change, but it is not clear that it is being rejected.[2]

It would seem rather far-fetched to expect a 'bottom-up' pupil-led revolution over ICT use in the near future. In fact there was a sense from some of the pupils in our study that they did not necessarily expect or even want to use ICT in schools in exactly the same manner as at home. In this respect, primary pupils should perhaps be seen as rather more discerning in their desire to use (and not use) ICTs than the idea of the digital native suggests. This was perhaps most apparent in children's discussions and drawings of future forms of technology-based schooling. Most of these ideas for change were surprisingly mundane and rooted in the present-day context of the classroom and existing structures of the school. Very few pupils imagined the 'blowing up' of the school or alternate 'virtual realities'. Instead, pupils' visions for change concerned mostly the addition of 'home' ICT devices and practices in the classroom, with little evident desire for change with a view to learning with ICTs.

Perhaps the most obviously desired change involved the relaxation of restrictions on ICT use imposed by the school – as many pupils put it in the discussion sessions and in their drawings, 'let us do what we want'. Of course, such demands echo the cries of 'it's not fair' that can often be heard from children on any manner of topics. Yet in the case of ICT these pleas highlight the especially unequal power relations that exist between pupils and their schools, their teachers, and their homes. Looking back over much of our data, we can see many instances where pupils' experiences of ICT were being shaped by school regulations and rules – not least in terms of the organizational pressures that schools face such as the delivery of curriculum content, time-tabling, filtering internet content and so on. In this sense, we can see how children's aspirations for changes to primary ICT were understandably influenced by the organizational contexts of schools in which they are located.

KEY ISSUE

The contentious nature of ICT change in primary education

Although many people are keen to see the improvement of ICT in schools, even the most innocuous suggestions for change are likely to face disagreement and resistance. Although ICT is generally accepted to be a 'good thing' in schools, a surprising number of people are fearful of the prospect of excessive technology change. Any teacher or head teacher attempting to follow this book's suggestions for the 'loosening up' of ICT is very likely to encounter a degree of scepticism and resistance from some parents and colleagues.

The strength of feeling against ICT change was highlighted when details of the Rose Report for reform of the primary curriculum hit the headlines in the British press in spring 2009. Despite the wide range of proposals contained in the Rose Report, press and public reaction focused on two main aspects – changes to the history curriculum and, in contrast, the addition of web 2.0 skills and literacies to the primary ICT curriculum.

The fact that the news media decided to seize upon Rose's proposals for ICT as their main 'story' says a lot about the symbolic role that technology plays in the way that society views schools and schooling. In particular, reactions to the Rose Report concentrated on the proposed promotion of high-tech skills and knowledge at the expense of traditional areas of teaching. The front-page headline in the *Guardian* newspaper said: 'Pupils to study *Twitter* and blogs in primary shakeup'. The *Daily Mail* announced: 'Exit Winston Churchill, enter Twitter ... Yes, it's the new primary school curriculum'.

These headlines led to a range of reaction from the education community. Some teaching unions and teacher organizations gave a cautious welcome to the changes in terms of flexibility and relevance to children's lives. As the head of the Association of Teachers and Lecturers commented: 'they are much more sensible programmes of study. We are pleased they give the profession much more flexibility to meet the needs of pupils. Children need to be enthused by learning, so they want to learn and gain the skills which will enable them to learn in later life'.[3]

Many people, however, were less welcoming – seeing the UK government as responding to a political pressure to 'keep up' with technological developments. As the head of the National Union of Teachers responded: 'It seems to jump on the latest trends such as Wikipedia and Twitter. ... Computer skills and keyboard skills seem to be as important as handwriting in this. Traditional books and written texts are downplayed in response to web-based learning.'[4]

On the whole, reactions to the headlines were surprisingly hostile – contrasting what most people saw as the trivial nature of web applications such as *Twitter* with the importance of learning about the British Empire and World War Two. As the *Daily Mail* chose to present the proposed changes:

> The new draft curriculum commissioned by the Government claims that pupils can do without learning about the battle against Nazism and the rise and fall of the British Empire ... In a move which will horrify many parents, it would see children focus on internet tools such as Wikipedia and podcasting, as well as innovations such as blogging and Twitter, which allows users to post minute-by-minute updates about their lives.[5]

As is the way with such news stories, perhaps the most revealing reactions were those from readers who subsequently wrote to newspapers and news websites in response to the stories. These reactions showed that members of the public – young and old – were generally appalled by the prospect of web 2.0 skills being given increased prominence within primary teaching. For some readers this represented an instance of the continued 'dumbing down' of school education and the teaching of 'fads that do not need to be taught'. Others argued that children would already have these skills and, if anything, should be teaching their teachers how to use *Twitter*. Even the former director of the University of London Institute of Education rubbished the proposals as yet another example of 'the crackpot schemes' introduced into education by badly advised politicians.[6] Very few people, if any, spoke up in favour of an expanded role for ICT skills, understandings and awareness to be featured in primary education.

Of course, such extreme reactions are to be expected from the type of person who offers responses to newspaper stories without having read the actual Curriculum Report (which had at the time only been leaked to one newspaper). But it would be wrong to dismiss these knee-jerk reactions, as they reflect a set of beliefs and opinions about primary ICT that is not usually voiced. However misinformed or politically motivated, we should remember that these are the responses of parents, grandparents, employers and teachers, and should be taken seriously.

Rethinking primary schools and ICT

What is perhaps most surprising about all of these findings is their ordinariness. In many ways this ordinariness should be seen as good news. It would seem that ICT is not especially different from any other aspect of pupils' experiences of primary education. As such, the state of ICT in primary schools today should not be seen as cause for particular concern *or* for particular celebration. In short, it would seem that there is not much more fundamentally wrong with primary ICT than there is with any other aspect of primary education. Compared to what we would have found in our study schools had we conducted our research five years earlier, ICT use appears to be in fairly good health. We found very few instances of pupils complaining about teachers not knowing about what they were doing with ICT. We found very few instances of pupils complaining about an absence of computers, internet connectivity or other resources. It could be said that we found clear signs of progress and 'e-maturity' across all of our study schools. Whereas ICT was still a novelty for many primary teachers at the beginning of the 2000s, it would now appear to be part of the fabric of primary education. That said, ICT could be characterized as a patchwork fabric – worn in places and lacking variety and sophistication.

As with all cases of maturity and stability, primary schools could now be said to be in danger of getting stuck in something of a rut when it comes to ICT. In many of our study schools the development of set patterns and perhaps even a declining sense of enthusiasm and excitement for ICT were noted. Left to their own devices, it is likely that all of the schools in our study would continue to 'get on' with ICT over the next five years in a similar fashion to before. While UK schools could be said to have come a long way with ICT since the days of the 'information superhighway' and the *National Grid for Learning*, there is a danger that the impetus and enthusiasm surrounding ICT in primary education are fading. So although things may have improved over the 2000s, there is still some way to go. In particular, we should remain mindful that just because children are now making more use of ICT in school, this does not mean that they could not be making *better* use of ICTs.

With these thoughts in mind, we conclude this book by giving some serious thought to how primary schools may be revitalized as sites of innovative and imaginative ICT use. It is clear from our study that a number of small improvements and adjustments can easily be made to primary ICT. We would not agree with the feelings amongst some educators and technologists that improvements to ICT in education will occur naturally as technology continues to develop. Our findings suggest that this is unlikely to be the case. Conversely, we do not believe that we have found primary ICT use to be in such a state of disrepair that drastic changes are required. We would not concur with the conclusions reached by many academic writers that schools simply do not appear to be 'up to the job' of educating children in the twenty-first century, and that we need a wholesale reinvention of primary education for the digital age.

Instead, we believe that anyone who is serious about improving primary ICT needs to be realistic about the primary school as it currently stands. Even the most enthusiastic education technologists must accept that primary schools are not about to change radically or disappear in the face of technology development. We must accept that primary schools are complex, messy and sometimes inefficient places. We must accept that primary teachers are often compromised and restricted in what they can do. With this realistic perspective in mind, it is perhaps most useful to use the remainder of this chapter to explore ways of improving ICT use that work *with* rather than *against* the 'big' pressures and priorities of primary education. In other words, we need to find ways of encouraging change that 'goes with the flow' of the primary school – for all its imperfections and frustrations.

Towards an agenda for change

How, then, should we pursue the technological 'loosening up' rather than a 'blowing up' of the primary school? Firstly, it would seem sensible to be modest and realistic about what can be done. Many of the unsatisfactory elements of primary ICT use highlighted in our study are rooted in far larger issues that cannot be addressed through technological changes alone. Many of the unsatisfactory elements of primary ICT use highlighted in this study are not issues about ICT *per se*, but about the general nature of schools and schooling. The fact that many pupils find ICT-based school work boring is not primarily due to the ways that ICT is presently being used, but to a wider disgruntlement with school work. Unless we are planning to radically alter the school system, then such issues will undoubtedly persist whatever technologies are developed.

Indeed, most of the children were rather more 'school-savvy' and accepting of the fact that ICT – like their clothing, food, and ability to go to the toilet – is controlled, monitored and regulated by school authorities. As such, unsatisfactory ICT use is just one of a number of disparities between what primary pupils would like and what primary pupils get. This could explain why most pupils offered relatively modest suggestions for changes to school ICT, such as 'using games' or 'MSN for ten minutes when good'. Most of these suggestions can be described as a temporary 'loosening up' of rules and regulations on an *ad hoc* basis. Perhaps, then, these pupils are being knowingly pragmatic and strategic in making such small-scale demands? Perhaps these pupils are being far more realistic than the many adult commentators who make far more extravagant but ultimately unrealistic demands for change? Could it be that these kinds of suggestions could be the most realistic and effective way of altering primary ICT?

It could be wise to try to 'think small' rather than 'thinking big' about any adjustments that can be made to primary ICT. In other words, we need to seek to make changes around the edges of the school in as unobtrusive a manner as possible. It seems to us that these should include changes that help ICT use 'fit' better with the realities of pupils' experiences of primary education. Where tensions and clashes relating to ICT were highlighted in our study, they were often related to a lack of 'goodness of fit' between ICT use and children's needs as pupils. In this sense changes could be made to alter the nature of ICT use in primary schools to fit better with the 'job' of being a pupil. As such, we would not suggest merely 'importing' popular, outside-school digital practices and artefacts into classrooms in the hope of transforming technology practices inside the school. As David Moseley and colleagues reason, 'giving pupils greater freedom to use computers in school in the same ways as they use them at home is unlikely to make any difference'.[7] In fact we do not see a need for primary schools to buy any new technology or for subject teachers to receive yet more training. Instead the answer to changing ICT use in school for the better could involve something as simple as changing the ways that schools talk about technology with their pupils. Here, then, are five proposals for change to primary ICT that follow this lead.

Five proposals for change

1. Establish a dialogic approach to ICT.
Here we are proposing that teachers and pupils enter into meaningful conversations about ICT and learning. This involves teachers talking *with* pupils about ICT, rather than just talking *to* them about ICT. Of course, many teachers will already do this for other aspects of their teaching. Finding out what learners know is fundamental to pedagogy – in a sense, all good teaching involves asking questions and talking with pupils.

2. Encourage a democratic approach to ICT.
Here we are proposing that 'cultures of trust' are developed between pupils and their schools with regard to ICT use. School rules and regulations can be decided through a 'negotiated governance' of technology use amongst all members of a school community. ICT rules and regulations can be based upon conditions of democracy and co-operation.

3. Encourage a 'loosening up' of ICT use wherever possible.
Here we are proposing that a more permissive use of children's personal ICTs is allowed in some of the quieter times, places and spaces around the edges of the school life. This would mean taking much greater advantage of the connectivity, portability and accessibility of children's personal and portable devices, whilst remaining mindful of inequalities in ownership.

4. Empower teachers to act as orchestrators and managers of pupils' ICT use.
Here we are proposing that teachers are given the confidence and skills to assume an active and authoritative role in informing, managing and directing the technological activities of their pupils. This will mean teachers getting deeply involved in all stages of pupils' ICT use in the classroom – rather than just 'setting them off and letting them get on with it'. This will mean teachers having a rich understanding and a 'feel' for the ICT applications that children will be using. This in turn will mean schools supporting the development of teachers' own use of ICT through their continuing professional development. Teachers can also explore opportunities to research their pupils' uses of ICTs in similar ways to our own research project, and share ideas and reflect on what works and what does not.

5. Develop children's 'critical digital literacy' alongside their 'media literacy'.
Here we are proposing that schools seek to develop pupils' creative skills and critical understandings required to make best use of technology in their everyday lives. This will mean helping children to think critically about their engagement with ICT, and connecting the teaching of ICT as a curriculum subject with emerging ways of thinking about media literacy and media education.

Taking it further – putting our ideas into action

We recognize that these options for change may still appear vague and lofty to some readers. In exploring each of the proposals in turn we can now offer a few simple suggestions as to how schools and teachers may like to go on from here, and put our ideas for the 'loosening up' of primary ICT into action.

Establishing a dialogic approach to ICT

Our first recommendation is that schools recognize the value of taking the time to talk with their pupils about ICT. We would recommend that schools enter into ongoing discussions between pupils, teachers and parents about ICT use. Teachers need to be encouraged to enter into meaningful conversations with pupils about ICT and learning – to talk *with* pupils about ICT, as well as talk *to* them about ICT. If teachers, ICT co-ordinators and school leaders are comfortable with listening to pupils' opinions, recommendations and experiences, than the benefits could be substantial.

Talking about ICT should be of benefit to a school community in at least three ways. The first is the opportunity for schools to get advice, ideas and guidance about ICT from their pupils. In short, pupils could act as an unofficial ICT advisory service or consultancy when it comes to how ICTs are used inside the school. Teachers should be encouraged and supported to explore alternative strategies of encouraging 'good' uses of ICTs in school that can draw upon the best elements of pupils' outside-school ICT use but retain an educational relevance and value.

Secondly, there is a clear role for schools to talk about how pupils may be using ICTs outside the school in ways that go beyond leisure and entertainment and have a more substantial – perhaps even educational – focus. In this sense schools can act as an initial point for children to be introduced to possible home ICT uses that go beyond games and passive consumption of online content. In short, teachers could act as guides for pupils when it comes to how ICTs are used outside school. In this sense we would argue that primary schools can be recast as sites of ICT exploration and recommendation rather than ICT restriction.

Thirdly, schools and teachers should be encouraged to foster informed dialogues with pupils about the educational benefits of using ICT inside school. We found little enthusiasm or excitement amongst the primary pupils in our study about ICT uses related to formal education. This suggests a clear need to enthuse children about learning with ICTs (and, in some cases, about learning in general) before any significant shifts in technology-supported learning can occur. Without some effort to 'sell' ICT-based learning in this way it is unlikely that children will force any 'bottom-up' change in schools' uses of ICTs for learning.

Pupils clearly have an important role to play in the development of future forms of school ICT use, but it would seem that teachers, school leaders and parents should take the lead in starting and steering these conversations. As a first step it would be worth considering whether such conversations have to take place in the context of ICT lessons or near any equipment at all. For example, might talking about ICT take place more regularly at registration time? Or might the conversations take place during class discussions within the context of the more active, pupil-centred rethinking of primary education conceived by the Rose Report?

Establishing a dialogic approach to ICT: Some ideas for classroom practice

1. Technology 'show and tell' sessions.
Sessions where pupils show the rest of the class a favourite website, application or device. Whilst demonstrating the technology, pupils can explain how they use it in their life, why they like it and what it means to them. Other class members can ask questions and discuss how they might like to use the technology of the day in school and at home. Teachers can also do the same.

2. If I were in charge...
Ask pupils to think about all of the children in the school, their needs, and the level of technology available to everyone. How would they organize the ICT in the school? What would they do which is radically different from how school ICT currently is arranged?

3. Topics for debate between pupils and teachers concerning new ways of teaching with and about ICTs.
- Do all lessons about ICT have to involve working with ICT? Can some involve thinking about ICT and discussing it, rather than actually using it?
- Which subjects may not always benefit from the use of ICT?
- Do ICT lessons always have to be in the ICT suite?
- In what ways can portable devices can be shared out between classes of pupils?
- Are there spaces and curriculum areas that are more appropriate for ICT use than others?

Encouraging a democratic approach to ICT

One of the main reasons for talking with pupils about ICT is to bring about a change to the cultures that surround ICT use in a school. By 'cultures' we mean shared understandings and expectations. These are often unspoken feelings and assumptions that people have about what ICT is and what it should (and should not) be used for. It is often difficult to identify or change school cultures, as they are built up over time and are often tacit – as can be seen in schools that are felt to have a distinct culture of sporting success or strict discipline. Yet it should be possible for school leaders and managers to be more aware of fostering feelings of exciting and expansive ICT use amongst everyone in a school. In particular, we would recommend that efforts be made to develop 'cultures of trust' between pupils and schools with regard to ICT use. In this sense the relations surrounding primary ICT will need to be moved on from the unease and mistrust that presently surround pupils' engagement with technology in some schools, to a set of more cooperative, consensual and civilized relations.

Perhaps the most obvious means of developing such trust is to allow a 'negotiated governance' of ICT use amongst all members of the school community. In short, ICT could be organized and regulated through democratic processes and co-operation between teachers and pupils. Rules, regulations and restrictions could be negotiated and decided on by everybody. The ways and means in which such negotiations could take place are now well established in many schools, such as whole 'school councils' of elected pupil representatives and daily classroom negotiations between individual teachers and their students. While the idea of school democracy is considered relevant to many aspects of school life (from encouraging dialogue on issues such as school meals, school uniforms and bullying), the topic of ICT use is not usually seen to be a suitable area for debate and negotiation. This oversight is surprising, as in-school ICT use would seem to be a highly appropriate topic for dialogue and debate between schools and pupils, especially given children's presumed interest in the area.

Pupils' involvement in the negotiation of school ICT could cover many different areas – from what items of hardware and software are purchased by the school to the nature of the blocks and filters that are placed on internet use. Above all, children could be allowed to negotiate the nature of the rules, regulations, structures and sanctions that currently shape ICT use within their school. As we saw throughout our project, in-school rules and regulations have a profound impact on how pupils experience ICT. The rules, regulations and other controls that surround ICT use would seem to be obvious areas for negotiation between all members of the school community. Pupils and teachers should be allowed to explore the leeway that exists for school rules to be relaxed or even ignored at certain times or in certain situations. The overall aim here would be to make ICT use in schools more of a self-governing process that is acceptable to pupils, teachers, parents and governors.

Whilst we know from Chapter 8 that some teachers and school leaders will see these suggestions as fraught with problems, there is little evidence from our study to suggest that primary-age children cannot be trusted to reach practical, responsible and realistic suggestions for technological change. As we have already noted, most of the pupils in our study displayed an acute awareness of the educational structures and requirements within which in-school ICT use is located. Many children appeared mindful of the risks involved in fully 'opening up' classroom settings and often seemed to share 'official' concerns over the 'usefulness' and 'safety' of unregulated technology use. We would argue that there are few reasons to suggest that allowing children an increased say in the governance of school ICT would result in a deluge of unreasonable or unrealistic demands. Although other areas of school democracy may well be more problematic and disruptive, perhaps ICT could be an area where increased trust in the opinions and actions of pupils is of real help to primary schools rather than a headache.

We would propose the setting up of pupil ICT 'interest groups', either within school councils or as standalone groups. These groups could be used to feed into discussions of all sorts of regulatory practices around the uses of ICT. We would suggest that far from threatening the e-safety of pupils, this participatory activity might actually protect them more – especially by developing their awareness and understanding of the issues.

Encouraging a democratic approach to ICT: some ideas for whole-school approaches

1. Place ICT policies on the agenda of *school councils*. Create a special interest group or separate committee from the school council specifically to discuss ICT on a regular basis.
2. Form an *ICT cabinet* made up of pupil volunteers to propose school policies and a school ICT manifesto. Let the children choose a pupil leader to chair the group.
3. Hold *ICT referenda* (across the whole school, a year group or whole class as appropriate) to vote on contentious topics or decisions to do with ICT use.
4. Appoint individual pupil volunteers as *investigative journalists* to report on the 'state of school technology' and the demands of the pupil body. In the spirit of the Rose Report, the texts that these journalists make should reflect the range of opportunities available to the children to extend their literacy skills. For example, in addition to being desktop-published to a high standard for an appropriate audience, the reports could be also presented as photo essays, video productions or podcasts.
5. Invite *ICT providers and gatekeepers* into the school to explain themselves to the pupils, and to discuss their actions – these could include representatives from the local authority or the school's managed learning provider.

Encouraging a democratic approach to ICT: some ideas for classroom practice

Topics for debate between pupils and teachers concerning the regulation of ICT:

- 'Wish-lists' of blocked websites and search terms
- 'Wish-lists' of unblocked websites and search terms
- Rules relating to where personal ICT use is allowed
- Rules relating to when personal ICT use is allowed
- Procurement policies – what devices and software should be purchased by the school for pupil use
- What personal ICT devices should be allowed into school.

Encouraging a 'loose use' of ICT

Assuming that conditions of trust and cooperation *can* be developed successfully within school communities, then it makes sense that pupils, teachers and school leaders focus their attention on the relaxing and 'loosening' of the boundaries that may constrain ICT use. These boundaries will be most apparent in terms of when, where and what kinds of technology use can take place. Such 'loosening' may include a number of areas of school ICT. For instance, attention could be given to the negotiated loosening of the types of ICT activities that are officially permitted or even unofficially tolerated within schools. From this perspective there may well be occasions to allow pupils to indulge in types of ICT activities that are not necessarily associated directly with the 'business' of schooling and learning, but nevertheless may provide a balance to more formal pedagogic and administrative uses of technology. These 'other' activities could include technology-based play and entertainment, informal communication and interaction with others, expressive activities and even the practices of simply 'hanging out' and 'messing around' with ICTs. Although not immediately productive, such activities could be seen as an important part of learning to use digital technology. School communities could even discuss the possible permission of the trivial uses of ICTs that are often banned or severely curtailed at present.

Many of these changes will involve rethinking the places, spaces and times within the school day where ICTs may be used. Instead of redesigning the architecture of the school and redrafting the timetable, this could simply involve searching for possibilities for the immediate adjustment 'around the edges' of the school building and school day. School communities could explore where informal ICT practices may be encouraged in otherwise quiet or 'slack times' of the school day such as lunchtimes, free times before and after school, and between lessons. Similar explorations could consider the 'loose spaces' within the physical environment of schools – spaces and places that have no prescribed formal pedagogic function, such as playgrounds, dining halls, entrance halls and corridors. It may also be that technology use can be encouraged in less obvious 'found spaces' within the school buildings and grounds – for example, stairwells, bicycle sheds and other hidden spaces of the school. This proposal could be used as an active part of the process of countering digital inequalities by increasing access at such times for children who do not have computers or handheld devices.

Encouraging a 'loose use' of ICT: some ideas for whole-school approaches

1. *Digital graffiti walls* – using plasma screens, digital projectors, whiteboards and so on to project pupil-created content onto public spaces. One example of this activity would be pupils text-messaging short slogans and phrases to appear temporarily on the walls of the playground, corridor or reception space. When these activities have been conducted with adults it is surprising how self-censoring people become. If schools are concerned, then pupils could be asked to vote on 'acceptable' use policies for what messages can and cannot be sent.
2. *Computer game Olympics* – competitive 'gamer' tournaments between pupils on games chosen by pupils. For example, devices such as *Wii Fit* could be used for *digital sports days*.
3. *'Old school' games tournaments* between teachers and pupils can be held, using games played by the teachers in their youth and therefore new to the pupils. Versions of old school games (also known as 'retro' games) can be easily found for free on online games sites such as *MiniClip*.
4. *Technology amnesty days* – allocated days in the school year when pupils can bring in any technology or media device that they wish, to play with or use in their free time. These should not just be the last days of term!

Encouraging a 'loose use' of ICT: some ideas for classroom practice

1. *'Suggest a technology' question*, to ask before starting any activity in the classroom. Scheduling in an in-class pause for thought before doing something. 'Is there anything you would like to use to do this?'
2. *Technology-free lessons* and *technology-rich lessons* – spontaneous decisions taken when appropriate to either spend the lesson using no new technology whatsoever *or else* as much technology as possible. These sessions can be akin to the 'let's work outside' decisions that sometime occur in the spring and summer time. Once the 'high-tech' or 'no-tech' sessions have finished, time can be taken to reflect upon what was good or what was not so good about the session.

Empowering teachers to become orchestrators and managers of pupils' ICT activities

Amidst all these dialogues, negotiations and relaxing of rules, we would stress that individual teachers should be given extra encouragement and extra opportunity to shape and direct pupils' use of ICT when in the classroom. There was little in our research findings to suggest that primary pupils are capable of making the most of ICT by themselves – with many highlighting their desire for some adult intervention or guidance. This is not to suggest that all teachers have to assume the mantle of being role models and 'gurus' of best technology practice. That said, teachers should be confident of the powerful role they play in introducing their pupils to ICT applications they may otherwise not come across. In this sense, teachers should be confident that they still have a valuable authoritative role in leading, managing and directing the techno-logical activities of their pupils.

As Charles Crook observes, the increasing complexity and sophistication of emerging ICTs such as web 2.0 applications brings 'significant distractions and obstructions' that children must confront.[8] In this sense, teachers can play important roles in supporting children's supposedly self-directed activities and providing the initial impetus for collaborative activities that underpin ICT-based learning. For example, it was clear from our study that many primary pupils would require considerable help and support to make effective use of the more difficult but more useful aspects of web 2.0 applications. In the case of technologies such as wikis and folksonomies, for example, there would seem to be ample scope for the orchestration of collaborative and communal activities, with teachers supplying a 'good core' and 'initial governance and impetus' necessary for any effective open collaboration.[9] There is no need for any teacher to feel unconfident about taking a lead in the classroom with ICT and supporting and scaffolding children's experiences of using such technologies. Neither should this development reside in the job description of one individual in the school. There is simply too much for ICT co-ordinators already to do in the way of managing resources and e-safety to give them sole responsibility.

For this proposal to work it will be important to ensure the provision of teachers' access to ICTs since, time and again, research has shown this to be a key factor in the confidence of teachers to develop innovative practice. Similarly, there is urgent need for continuing professional development for all teachers – not just those who are leading ICT in school. ICT training and development could perhaps be linked into the general moves throughout the school sector towards master's level education for all teachers. There are also opportunities to allow teachers to participate in less formal, non-accredited short courses or support groups. In particular, such provision could address ICT from different curriculum standpoints, reflecting the interests which some teachers have in creative media production or online activities which are driven by an interest in literacy and what children are capable of making and publishing, more than any specific technological focus.

Empowering teachers to become orchestrators and managers: some ideas for teacher practice

1. Encourage teachers to undertake professional development and to share their ideas for changing practice. This will require some investment on the part of schools, perhaps encouraging teachers to take shorter, practical courses, for example in aspects of media production or in other ways of engaging with children's media and, where appropriate, to think about extending skills and reflection at master's level.

2. Encourage teachers to share successful ideas for implementing changes with each other. This can take place formally in staff meetings, as well as informally at other times. Such exchanges should be truly cross-curricular and enabling in nature – not residing solely in the domain of the ICT expert(s) in the school.

3. Teachers of all subjects should be encouraged to show each other the uses of media technologies in their areas. Digital video production, for example, is a tool that could be used across the curriculum in explorations of new media with pupils that will build connections with their interests outside school and generally impact on how ICT is perceived and used by the school community. Examples of ICTs in use across the curriculum could build shared confidence and expertise: literacy co-ordinators leading in the production of short video pieces or animation; science co-ordinators showing how they can use simple monitoring devices in their work; early years practitioners sharing their use of digital photography and audio recordings in record-keeping.

4. Parents can be invited to support the uses of ICT in a range of activities where they can share expertise with all users. These areas of ICT use could include parents' own uses of digital photography; how they manage their music collections; where ICT is part of their professional life and so on. Partnership with parents in this way may be encouraged via a 'technology week' or 'media week' in school.

5. Teachers can be encouraged to 'play' with ICTs in staff directed time, such as staff meetings and INSET days. Perhaps one staff meeting a term (or more) could be designated as a digital media experience. This could involve teachers in making media or playing video games, demonstrating uses of social networking sites to less experienced members of staff. This would bring teachers into direct personal contact with the skills and dispositions of their pupils. Such sessions could generate empathy by positioning teachers as learners and challenging teachers with tasks beyond their usual comfort zones. If nothing else, teachers would have something on which to base the conversations suggested above in our first proposal for change.

Developing children's 'critical digital literacy' alongside their 'media literacy'

Our final proposal concerns the need for schools to ensure that pupils are informed about their choices and actions when using ICTs – what could be termed their 'critical digital literacies'. 'Critical digital literacy' can be seen as involving a lot more than just keyboard skills and awareness of 'e-safety'. Instead, it involves helping children develop a full range of creative abilities to make use of ICT, alongside the critical understandings required to make best use of ICTs. There is potential here for joining primary ICT with the emergent media literacy curriculum. The UK government's own definition of media literacy, provided by Ofcom, described this as 'the ability to access, understand and create communications in a variety of contexts'.[10]

In terms of the creative skills and abilities of the pupils in our study, there were many areas of ICT use and media literacy that could be improved. Henry Jenkins, for example, proposes a list of 'new literacy skills' to consider in thinking about how schools teach their pupils about ICT.[11] It is interesting to reflect upon how many of these skills primary pupils are currently able to develop through their school use of ICT:

- *play* – the capacity to experiment with one's surroundings as a form of problem-solving;
- *performance* – the ability to adopt alternative identities for the purpose of improvisation and discovery;
- *appropriation* – the ability to meaningfully 'sample' and 'remix' online content;

- *collective intelligence* – the ability to pool knowledge and compare notes with others toward a common goal;
- *transmedia navigation* – the ability to follow the flow of stories and information across different forms of ICT;
- *networking* – the ability to search for, synthesize, and disseminate information.

Besides these creative skills, perhaps the most important capacity that pupils should be encouraged to develop is a critical thinking about ICT itself. The area of creative thinking is a growing part of the primary curriculum, and it could be argued that the development of better critical understandings of ICTs underpins the success of all the other suggestions for change that we have outlined up until now. As Kay Withers notes, 'the success of self- and co-regulation relies on users themselves being able to make informed decisions: being "media literate" in the way they access and use content and information'.[12] In this sense, it should be possible for teachers to help their pupils question and challenge the place of ICT in their everyday lives.

A critical thinking approach would be an ideal means, for example, of helping pupils discuss issues of e-safety and 'appropriate' uses of technology – moving their understandings away from what Shirley Alexander recently called the unhelpful and seemingly ineffectual 'hard-hitting messages' that merely serve to add 'to a culture of fear that doesn't help our young people'.[13] Critical thinking could also help children to get to grips with the many non-technical challenges and issues associated with using ICTs – not least issues such as discerning the authenticity and academic authority of online information and 'facts', as well as issues of 'privacy' and 'trust' when using the internet. When helping pupils develop ICT skills, schools should be mindful that there is a lot more to think about than which button to press and which icon to click on. These additional complex aspects are all addressed by having a critical conception of what it means to be literate and skilled in the twenty-first century.

Developing children's 'critical digital literacy': some ideas for whole-school approaches

Using anonymous confession boxes in school, where children can post instances of and experiences with ICT that have concerned them. These can form the basis of discussions in class and in school assemblies.

Developing children's 'critical digital literacy': some ideas for class activities

1. Scrutinizing Wikipedia. Children could be helped to understand that a wiki application such as *Wikipedia* is an ongoing process written by many different people not a static product written by one expert.

Step one – 'Acting out the Wikipedia process on the board'
- Chose a topic that all pupils are able to write a description of.
- Ask all pupils to write a five-line description. The teacher should write their own description on the board.
- Ask pupils to point out bits of the teacher's description on the board that they feel are wrong, or could be made better. Rub out and replace the original definition as the group sees fit.
- Continue this process of debating and deleting until most people in the class are happy with the description.
- Compare and contrast the final definition and the original version. Discuss what is better about the final version, and what may have changed or been lost in all of the corrections.

Step two – 'Looking at the Wikipedia process on the computer'
- Look up the Wikipedia definition of your chosen topic – compare it to the definition the class developed on the board.
- Click on the 'Discussion' tab at the top left-hand corner of the Wikipedia page to see the discussion amongst the Wikipedia contributors and editors.
- Click on the 'History' tab at the top left-hand corner of the Wikipedia page to see history of the definition and when it was changed. Count the number of people involved in its writing.

NB. If your chosen topic has not been the subject of much interest on Wikipedia then also look at the 'Discussion' and 'History' sections of a more active topic – such as Harry Potter, Barack Obama or your local football team.

Step three – 'Adding to Wikipedia on the computer'
If there is interest then pupils could be involved in attempting to add some content to Wikipedia. The whole class could do this – with the teacher or an older child acting as the contributor on an interactive whiteboard. A good topic to either create (or add to if it already exists)

is a brief entry on your local area. Once the material has been added, check back after a week or two to see what has happened!

2. *Making autobiographical media pieces.* Encourage the children at transition points at the end of Key Stages 1 and 2 to undertake reflective practices with digital video and audio, making short autobiographical pieces about their time at the school. This practice has been shown to be effective in engaging with children's experience of media culture and with new literacies in moving-image and still-image form. Activities like this generally mean a higher level of engagement with a critical media literacy practice and enable useful and constructive discussions to take place, positioning learners as producers of media and not merely consumers.

3. *Holding class debates about e-safety issues in the news*, where children and teachers discuss media stories about young people and technology. How balanced are the views put forward? How likely do you think these experiences are to occur to you?

What to do now?

All of these recommendations are concerned with different ways of 'democratizing' the use of ICT in primary education. Although this sounds like a high-minded and unrealistic ambition, we hope that this chapter has provided some sense of what changes could be made. In short, we are proposing that schools explore their options for relaxing and de-restricting the expectations, guidelines, rules and regulations that surround ICT use. It is perhaps important to emphasize again that we are not proposing the deregulation of primary ICT use into some form of digital 'free-for-all'. Instead we are seeking to encourage changes 'around the edges' of the primary school. These are changes that may allow forms of ICT engagement that are richer and more meaningful to children, yet pose minimal threat to the overall order and wider organizational priorities of the school. As such, serious thought now needs to be given to how children's in-school ICT use can be refined in ways that *complement* rather than *challenge* the 'big' priorities and pressures of curriculum, assessment, education policy and so on.

We realize that making any of these adjustments and alterations will not be easy. We were certainly reminded of the many difficulties of changing school ICT by the 'teacher voices' described in Chapter 8. It is therefore important to expect any refinements and changes to school technology use to be incremental and gradual. Having made our recommendations, we remain aware that primary schools are highly controlled and regulated places, and that any change is likely to be slow and gradual. Yet we also remain confident that such changes are possible if the majority of people within a school community are ready and willing to help change the culture of school ICT. This will require teachers to be ready to listen to pupil perspectives and perhaps even compromise a little. If the 'in through the backdoor' approaches to ICT change that we are advocating in this book are to be successful, then talking with children about their technology use would appear to be an obvious and essential place to start.

As we have seen throughout this book, ICT is a conversation that everyone within a school needs to join – especially pupils and teachers. From our experiences of conducting our research project, we are convinced that ICT is a suitable and fruitful topic of conversation for any primary school. Talking about technology should be an easy thing to include in day-to-day activities of primary school. Children will have many things to say, and teachers will be engaged in activities that are all now being given a heightened role in primary education through the promotion of 'oracy' in the primary curriculum – especially developing debating, public speaking and communication skills.

School communities need to initiate conversations that are not only about 'how to' use ICT, but also 'why to' use ICT. Indeed, one of the first steps to change is enthusing and convincing everyone about the need to use ICT in schools. Only when there is some degree of consensus about why ICT is a good thing in schools can meaningful changes occur. Establishing a sense of consensus, co-operation and collective responsibility around primary ICT is perhaps our most important conclusion. ICT change will not be completely 'bottom-up' from the current generation of 'digital natives'. Neither can ICT changes be completely imposed 'top-down' from school authorities. Pupils and teachers need to work together if ICTs are to be used in primary schools in more meaningful, effective and perhaps even more enjoyable ways.

This chapter has attempted to advance a modest case for exploring ways of 'loosening up' school ICT use and introducing a degree of informality to primary ICT without undermining the overall institutionalized social order of the school. Of course, many of the education technology experts and commentators high-lighted in the opening chapters of this book may well consider this to be a disappointingly compromised agenda for change. Yet we feel that our conclusions are certainly more realistic and achievable than the radical conclusions on offer elsewhere. To reiterate, we are not calling for school use of technology to be allowed to descend into an ultimately ineffectual free-for-all. Instead, we believe that primary schools should now set about experimenting with ways in which a beneficial loosening of ICT use may be achieved 'around the edges' of the school. Crucially, this depends on allowing pupils a greater say in primary ICT.

Notes and references

Chapter 1: The 'big' priorities and pressures of primary ICT

1   Suppes, P. (1965) Computer-assisted instruction in the schools: potentialities, problems, prospects. Technical Report 81. Stanford University, Institute for Mathematical Studies in the Social Sciences (http://suppes-corpus.-stanford.edu/techreports/IMSSS_81.pdf).

2   Cuban, L., Kirkpatrick, H. and Peck, C. (2001) 'High access and low use of technology in high school classrooms: explaining an apparent paradox', *American Educational Research Journal*, 38, 4, 813–834.

3   Dylan Willam, speech to Institute of Fiscal Studies conference, Cambridge, cited in BBC News Online (2009) 'Class equipment can be a waste', 2 April (http://news.bbc.co.uk/1/hi/education/7976680.stm).

4   Apple, M. (2004) 'Are we wasting money on computers in schools?', *Educational Policy*, 18, 3, 513–522.

5   Laurillard, D. (2008) *Digital Technologies and their Role in Achieving our Ambitions for Education*. London: Institute of Education (p. 1).

6   Boody, R. (2001) 'On the relationships of education and technology', in R. Muffoletto (ed.) *Education and Technology: Critical and Reflective Practices*. Cresskill, NJ: Hampton Press.

7   Surowiecki, J. (2004) *The Wisdom of Crowds: Why the Many are Smarter than the Few and how Collective Wisdom Shapes Business, Economies, Societies and Nations*. New York: Little Brown

8   Prenksy, M. (2001) 'Digital natives, digital immigrants', *On the Horizon*, 9, 5, 1–6 (p. 1).

9   Rideout, V. and Hammel, E. (2006) *The Media Family*. Menlo Park, CA: Kaiser Family Foundation.

    Rideout, V., Roberts, D. and Foehr, U. (2005) *Generation M: Media in the Lives of 8–18 Year-Olds*. Menlo Park, CA: Kaiser Family Foundation.

    Veen, W. and Vrakking, B. (2006) *Homo Zappiens: Growing Up in a Digital Age*. London: Continuum.

10 Fisher, M. and Baird, D. (2009) 'Pedagogical mashup: gen Y, social media, and digital learning styles', in L. Hin and R. Subramaniam, R. (eds) *Handbook of Research on New Media Literacy at the K-12 Level*. Hershey, PA: IGI Global.

11 Prensky, M. (2005) 'Listen to the natives', *Educational Leadership* 63, 4, 8–13 (p. 8).

12 Tapscott, D. and Williams, A. (2007) *Wikinomics: How Mass Collaboration Changes Everything*. New York: Atlantic.

13 Palfrey, J. and Gasser, U. (2008) *Born Digital: Understanding the First Generation of Digital Natives*. New York: Basic.

   Veen and Vrakking, *Homo Zappiens*.

   Levin, D. and Arafeh, S. (2002) *The Digital Disconnect*. Washington, DC: Pew Internet and American Life Project.

14 Vandewater, E., Rideout, V., Wartella, E., Huang, X., Lee, J. and Shim, M. (2007) 'Digital childhood', *Pediatrics*, 119, 5, 1006–1015.

   Pedró, F. (2007) 'The New Millennium Learners', *Nordic Journal of Digital Literacy*, 2, 4, 244–264.

   Rideout and Hammel, *The Media Family*.

15 Holloway, S. and Valentine, G. (2003) *Cyberkids: Children in the Information Age*. London: Routledge (p. 30).

16 Christine Gilbert, cited in BBC News Online (2009) 'Slump in school computer lessons', 3 March (http://news.bbc.co.uk/go/pr/fr/-/1/hi/education/7919350.stm).

17 New Zealand Government (2008) *The Draft Digital Strategy 2.0: Achieving our Digital Potential*. Wellington: Ministry of Economic Development (p. 23).

18 Paton, G. (2009) 'Primary schoolchildren will learn to read on Google in "slimmer" curriculum', *Daily Telegraph*, 30 April.

19 Rose, J. (2009) *Independent Review of the Primary Curriculum: Final Report*. London: Department of Children, Schools and Families (p. 12).

20 Alexander, R. and Flutter, J. (2009) *Towards a New Primary Curriculum: A Report from the Cambridge Primary Review. Part One: Past and Present*. Cambridge: Cambridge University Faculty of Education (p. 30).

21 Alexander and Flutter, *Towards a New Primary Curriculum, Part One* (p. 30).

22 Alexander, R. and Flutter, J. (2009) *Towards a New Primary Curriculum: A Report from the Cambridge Primary Review. Part Two: The Future*. Cambridge: Cambridge University Faculty of Education.

23 Jim Rose, cited in S. Dodson (2009) 'Make the most of tech-savvy tots', *Guardian*, 13 January, Resource 2009 supplement, p. 2.

24 Jim Knight, cited in J. Schofield, J. (2009) 'Technology starts at home', *Guardian*, 13 January, Resource 2009 supplement, p. 3.

25 Mason, R. and Rennie, F. (2007) 'Using web 2.0 for learning in the community', *Internet and Higher Education*, 10, 196–203 (p. 199).

26 Nichol, J., Watson, K. and Waites, G. (2003) 'Rhetoric and reality: using ICT to

enhance pupil learning – Harry Potter and the Warley Woods Mystery'. *British Journal of Educational Technology*, 34, 2, 201–213.

27   Passey, D., Rogers, C., Machell, J., McHugh, G. and Allaway, D. (2004) *The Motivational Effect of ICT on Pupils*. Nottingham: Department for Education and Skills.

28   Withers, K. with Sheldon, R. (2008) *Behind the Screen: The Hidden Life of Youth Online*. London: Institute for Public Policy Research.

29   Byron, T. (2008) *Safer Children in a Digital World* (The Byron Review). Nottingham: Department for Children, Schools and Families, and the Department for Culture, Media and Sport (www.dcsf.gov.uk/byronreview).

30   ISTTF (2008) *Enhancing Child Safety & Online Technologies: Final Report of the Internet Safety Technical Task Force to the Multi-State Working Group on Social Networking of State Attorneys General of the United States*. Harvard University, Berkman Centre for Internet and Society (http://cyber.law.harvard.edu/research/isttf).

31   Ball, S. (2003) 'The teacher's soul and the terrors of performativity', *Journal of Educational Policy*, 18, 2, 215–228.

Chapter 2: The promises and problems of primary ICT

1   Prenksy, M. (2001) 'Digital natives, digital immigrants', *On the Horizon*, 9, 5, 1–6.

2   Small, G. and Vorgon, G. (2008) *iBRAIN: Surviving the Technological Alteration of the Modern Mind*. London: Collins.

3   Prensky, M. (2008) 'Backup education?', *Educational Technology*, 48, 1, January/February.

4   Wales, J. (2008) 'It's the next billion online who will change the way we think', *Observer*, 15 June, p. 23.

5   Davies, P. (1998) 'Formalising learning: the role of accreditation'. Paper presented to ESRC Learning Society seminar, Bristol.

6   Jim Knight, cited in Woodward, W. (2008) 'Plan to give every child internet access at home', *Guardian*, 4 January, p. 2.

7   Schmitta, J. and Wadsworth, J. (2006) 'Is there an impact of household computer ownership on children's educational attainment in Britain?', *Economics of Education Review*, 25, 6, 659–673.

Madden, A., Ford, N., Miller, D. and Levy, P. (2005) 'Using the internet in teaching: the views of practitioners', *British Journal of Educational Technology*, 36, 2, 255–280.

Becker, H. (2000) 'Findings from the teaching, learning and computing survey: is Larry Cuban right?', in *The Proceedings of the 2000 State Education Technology Conference*. Washington, DC: Council of Chief State School Officers.

Brush, T. (1999) 'Technology planning and implementation in public schools', *Computers in the Schools*, 15, 2, 11–23.

8   Angrist, J. and Lavy, V. (2002) 'New evidence on classroom computers and pupil learning', *Economic Journal*, 112, 735–765.

Fuchs, T. and Woessmann, L. (2004) 'What accounts for international differences in student performance? A re-examination using PISA data', *Econometric Society 2004 Australasian Meetings* 274, Econometric Society.

Lauven, E., Lindahl, M., Oosterbeek, H. and Webbink, D. (2003) 'The effect of extra funding for disadvantaged students on achievement'. Department of Economics, University of Amsterdam.

Dynarski, M., Agodini, R., Heaviside, S., Novak, T., Carey, N. and Campuzano, L. (2007). *Effectiveness of Reading and Mathematics Software Products: Findings from the First Student Cohort* (Publication No. 2007–4005). Washington, DC: Institute of Education Sciences, US Department of Education.

9   Foehr, U. (2006) *Media Multitasking among American Youth: Prevalence, Predictors and Pairings*. Menlo Park, CA: Henry J. Kaiser Family Foundation.

Wallis, C. (2006) 'The multitasking generation', *Time*, 167, 48–55.

10   Tapscott, D. and Williams, A. (2007) *Wikinomics: How Mass Collaboration Changes Everything*. New York: Atlantic (p. 47).

11   Leadbeater, C. (2008) *We-think*. London: Profile (p. 36).

12   Solomon, G. and Schrum, L. (2007) *Web 2.0: New Tools, New Schools*. Washington, DC: International Society for Technology in Education (p. 8).

13   Keen, A. (2007) *The Cult of the Amateur*. London: Nicholas Brealey (p. 93).

14   Keen, *The Cult of the Amateur* (p. 25).

15   Sigman, A. (2009) 'Well connected', *The Biologist*, 56, 1, 14–20.

Harkin, J. (2009) *Cyburbia: The Dangerous Idea that's Changing How We Live and Who We Are*. London: Little, Brown.

16   Susan Greenfield, cited in Lords Hansard (2009) 'Children: Social Networking Sites: Debate', *Lords Hansard*, vol. 707, no. 33 (12 February) cols 1290–1293 (www.publications.parliament.uk/pa/ld200809/ldhansrd/index/090212.html).

17   Bugeja, M. (2006) 'Facing the Facebook', *Chronicle of Higher Education*, 52, 21, January 27, p. C1.

18   Alan Johnson, speech to the NASUWT Annual Conference (2007), Belfast, 10 April.

19   BBC News (2009) 'Call to give up texting for Lent', *BBC News Online*, 4 March.

20   British Educational Suppliers Association (2008) *BESA Report: BESA ICT in UK State Schools 2008*. London: BESA.

21 Barker, R. and Gardiner, J. (2007) *'e-learning and e-skills'*, in V. Avery, E. Chamberlain, C. Summerfield and L. Zealey (eds), *Focus on the Digital Age*. London: Office for National Statistics (www.statistics.gov.uk/downloads/theme_compendia/foda2007/Chapter3.pdf).

British Educational Suppliers Association (2008) *Information and Communication Technology in UK State Schools*. London: BESA.

22 Laurillard, D. (2008) *Digital Technologies and their Role in Achieving our Ambitions for Education*. London: Institute of Education (p. 34).

23 Crowne, S. (2007) 'Keynote speech' presented to Harnessing Technology: Delivering the Future for Learners: North East Regional Conference, Newcastle, 15 March.

24 Moseley, D., Mearns, N. and Tse, H. (2001) 'Using computers at home and in the primary school: where is the value added?', *Educational & Child Psychology*, 18, 3, 31–46.

Tondeur, J., van Braak, J. and Valcke, M. (2007) 'Primary school curricula and the use of ICT in education: Two worlds apart?', *British Journal of Educational Technology*, 38, 962–975.

Tondeur, J., van Braak, J. and Valcke, M. (2007) 'Towards a typology of computer use in primary education', *Journal of Computer Assisted Learning*, 23, 3, 197–206.

Hall, I. and Higgins, S. (2005) 'Primary school students' perceptions of interactive whiteboards', *Journal of Computer Assisted Learning* 21, 2, 102–117.

Waite, S., Wheeler, S. and Bromfield, C. (2007) 'Our flexible friend: The implications of individual differences for information technology', *Computers & Education*, 48, 1, 80–99.

Wall, K., Higgins, S. and Smith, H. (2005) '"The visual helps me understand the complicated things": pupil views of teaching and learning with interactive whiteboards', *British Journal of Educational Technology*, 36, 5, 851–867.

25 Bigum, C. and Rowan, L. (2008) 'Landscaping on shifting ground', *Asia-Pacific Journal of Teacher Education*, 36, 3, 245–255 (p. 249).

26 Kenway, J. and Bullen, E. (2005) 'Globalising the young in the age of desire: some educational policy issues', in M. Apple, J. Kenway, and M. Singh (eds) *Globalising Public Education: Policies, Pedagogies and Politics*. New York: Peter Lang.

27 Madden, A., Nunes, J., McPherson, M., Ford, N., Miller, D. and Rico, M. (2005) 'A new generation gap? Some thoughts on the consequences of increasingly early ICT first contact', *International Journal of Information and Communication Technology Education*, 1, 2, 19–33.

Levin, D. and Arafeh, S. (2002) *The Digital Disconnect*. Washington, DC: Pew Internet and American Life Project.

28   Green, B. and Bigum, C. (1993) 'Aliens in the classroom', *Australian Journal of Education*, 37, 2, 119–141.

29   Long, S. (2005) 'Digital natives: if you aren't one, get to know one', *New Library World*, 106, 3–4, 187–189.

30   Prensky, M. (2005) 'Listen to the natives', *Educational Leadership* 63, 4, 8–13 (p. 8).

31   Dale, R., Robertson, S. and Shortis, T. (2004) '"You can't not go with the technological flow, can you?" Constructing "IT" and teaching and learning: the interaction of policy, management and technology', *Journal of Computer Assisted Learning*, 20, 456–470.

32   Keen, *The Cult of the Amateur* (p. 201).

33   Heppell, S., Chapman, C., Millwood, R., Constable, M. and Furness, J. (2004) *'Building learning futures...'.* CABE / RIBA 'Building Futures' programme (pp. 41–43).

34   Perelman, L. (1992) *School's Out: Hyperlearning, the New Technology, and the End of Education*. New York: Avon

35   Papert, S. (1984) 'Trying to predict the future', *Popular Computing*, October.

36   Papert, S. (1998) 'Does easy do it? Children, games, and learning', *Game Developer*, June/September, p. 88.

37   Papert, 'Does easy do it?'.

38   Castells, M. (2008) 'Internet beyond myths: the record of scholarly research'. Presentation to London School of Economics, 24 October.

39   Negroponte, N. (1995) *Being Digital*. London: Coronet.

      Shaffer, D. (2008) 'Education in the digital age', *Nordic Journal of Digital Literacy*, 4, 1, 39–51.

40   Jenkins, H. (2006) *Confronting the Challenges of Participatory Culture: Media Education for the 21st Century*. Chicago: MacArthur Foundation.

41   Leadbeater, *We-think* (p. 149).

42   Toffler, A. (1970) *Future Shock*. London: Bodley Head.

43   Luke, C. (2003) 'Pedagogy, connectivity, multimodality and interdisciplinarity', *Reading Research Quarterly*, 38, 397–403 (p. 398).

44   Leadbeater, *We-think* (p. 147).

45   Prensky, M. (2008) 'The role of technology in teaching and the classroom', *Educational Technology*, 48.

46   Tapscott, D. (1999) 'Educating the net generation', *Educational Leadership*, 56, 5, 6–11 (p. 11).

47   Kerr, S. (1996) 'Toward a sociology of educational technology', in D. Jonassen (ed.) *Handbook of Research on Educational Communications and Technology*. New York: Macmillan (p. 7).

48   Sefton-Green, J. (2004) *Informal Learning with Technology outside School.* Bristol: Futurelab (p. 32).

Chapter 3: Getting a pupil perspective – description of our research study

1   Withers, K. with Sheldon, R. (2008) *Behind the Screen: The Hidden Life of Youth Online.* London: Institute for Public Policy Research.

2   Comber, C., Watling, R., Lawson, T., Cavendish, S. and McEune, C. (2003) *ImpaCT2 Learning at Home and School.* London: Department for Education and Skills (p. 38).

3   Department for Education and Skills (2004) *Five Year Strategy for Children and Learners.* London: Stationery Office.

4   Bragg, S. (2007) *Consulting Young People: A Review of the Literature.* London: Creative Partnerships.

5   Fielding, M. (2001) 'Students as radical agents of change', *Journal of Educational Change,* 2, 123–141.

6   Robinson, C. and Fielding, M. (2007) *Children and their Primary Schools: Pupils' Voices.* Cambridge: Cambridge University Faculty of Education.

7   Ito, M., Horst, H., Bittanti, M., Boyd, D., Herr-Stephenson, R., Lange, P., Pascoe, C. and Robinson, L. (2008) *Living and Learning with New Media.* Chicago: MacArthur Foundation (p. 35).

8   Levin, D. and Arafeh, S. (2002) *The Digital Disconnect.* Washington, DC: Pew Internet and American Life Project.

9   Strauss, A. (1987) *Qualitative Analysis for Social Scientists.* Cambridge: Cambridge University Press.

Chapter 4: *PowerPoint* and penguins – primary pupils' use of ICTs at school and at home

1   Allan, K. (2009) 'Hey kids! Wanna play an MMORPG?', *Guardian,* 9 April, Technology supplement, p. 5.

2   Sung Jin Kim, cited in Allan, 'Hey kids! Wanna play an MMORPG?'.

Chapter 5: Allowing primary pupils to speak for themselves about ICT

1   Jeffrey, R. and Woods, P. (1997) 'The relevance of creative teaching: pupil's views', in A. Pollard, D. Thiessen, and A. Filer (eds) *Children and their Curriculum: The Perspectives of Primary and Elementary School Children.* London: Falmer.

2   Miller, D. and Robertson, D. (2010) 'Using a games console in the primary classroom: effects of "Brain Training" programme on computation and self-esteem', *British Journal of Educational Technology* (forthcoming).

3   Smithers, R. (2009) 'Which? panel questions brain training claims', *Guardian*, 26 February, p. 5.

Chapter 6: Drawing digital pictures: primary pupils' representations of the future of school ICT

1   Mavers, D. (2003) 'Communicating meanings through image composition, spatial arrangement and links in primary school student mind maps', in C. Jewitt and G. Kress (eds) *Multimodal Literacy*. New York: Peter Lang (p. 20).

2   Topping, A. (2007) 'Children bond with their robot playmates', *Guardian*, 6 November.

Chapter 7: Primary pupils' experiences and understandings of 'e-safety'

1   Palmer, S. (2006) *Toxic Childhood: How the Modern World is Damaging our Children and What We Can Do about it*. London: Orion.

2   Nairn, A. and Mayo, E. (2009) *Consumer Kids*. London: Constable.

3   Berson, I., Berson, M. and Ferron, J. (2002) 'Emerging risks of violence in the digital age', *Journal of School Violence*, 1, 2, 51–72 (p. 52).

4   Becta (2006) *Safeguarding children in a digital world*. Coventry: British Educational Communications and Technology Agency (p. 10).

5   Byron, T. (2008) *Safer children in a digital world (The Byron Review)*. Nottingham: Department for Children, Schools and Families, and the Department for Culture, Media and Sport (www.dcsf.gov.uk/byronreview).

6   Valcke, M., Schellens, T., Van Keer, H. and Gerarts, M. (2007) 'Primary school children's safe and unsafe use of the Internet at home and at school: an exploratory study', *Computers in Human Behavior*, 23, 6, 2838–2850 (p. 2848).

7   Ybarra, M., Mitchell, K., Wolak, J. and Finkelhor, D. (2006) 'Examining characteristics and associated distress related to internet harassment', *Pediatrics* 118, 4, e1169–e1177

8   O'Connell, R., Sange, S. and Barrow, C. (2002) *Young People's Use of Chat Rooms*. Preston: University of Central Lancashire.

9   Mediappro (2006) *The Appropriation of New Media by youth: End of Project Report*. Leuven: Catholic University of Louvain (www.mediappro.org/publications/finalreport.pdf)

10   Livingstone, S. (2003) 'Children's use of the internet: reflections on the emerging research agenda', *New Media and Society*, 5, 2, 147–167.

Chapter 9: Suggestions for changing primary ICT

1   Withers, K. with Sheldon, R. (2008) *Behind the Screen: The Hidden Life of Youth Online*. London: Institute for Public Policy Research (p. 41).

2 Bennett, S., Maton, K. and Kervin, L. (2008) 'The "digital natives" debate', *British Journal of Educational Technology*, 39, 5, 775–786 (p. 783).

3 Mary Bousted, cited in P. Curtis (2009) 'Pupils to study Twitter and blogs in primary shake-up', *Guardian*, 27 March, pp. 1–2 (p. 2).

4 John Bangs, cited in Curtis, 'Pupils to study Twitter and blogs in primary shake-up' (p. 1).

5 Cohen, T. (2009) 'Exit Winston Churchill, enter Twitter … Yes, it's the new primary school curriculum', *Daily Mail*, Online, 27 March.

6 Mortimore, P. (2009) 'Let's end these crackpot schemes', *Guardian*, 7 April, Education supplement, p. 4.

7 Moseley, D., Mearns, N., and Tse, H. (2001) 'Using computers at home and in the primary school: where is the value added?', *Educational & Child Psychology*, 18, 3, 31–46 (p. 45).

8 Crook, C. (2008) 'Theories of formal and informal learning in the world of web 2.0', in S. Livingstone (ed.) *Theorising the Benefits of New Technology for Youth*. University of Oxford and London School of Economics.

9 Leadbeater, C. (2008) *We-think*. London: Profile.

10 Ofcom (2005) *Ofcom's Strategy and Priorities for the Promotion of Media Literacy – a statement*. London: Office of Communications.

11 Jenkins, H. (2006) *Confronting the Challenges of Participatory Culture: Media Education for the 21st Century*. Chicago: MacArthur Foundation (p. 4)

12 Withers, *Behind the Screen* (p. 51).

13 Shirley Atkinson, cited in J. Nightingale (2009) 'Don't panic!', *Guardian*, 13 January, Resource 2009 supplement, p. 8.

Index

DATE DUE

GAYLORD   PRINTED IN U.S.A.

LB 1028.3 .S3888 2010

Selwyn, Neil.

Primary schools and ICT